LET ME LIE

Books by James Branch Cabell

BALLADES FROM THE HIDDEN WAY • BEYOND LIFE • THE
CERTAIN HOUR • CHIVALRY • THE CORDS OF VANITY • THE
CREAM OF THE JEST • DOMNEI • THE EAGLE'S SHADOW •
FIGURES OF EARTH • THE FIRST GENTLEMAN OF AMERICA •
FROM THE HIDDEN WAY • GALLANTRY • HAMLET HAD AN
UNCLE • THE HIGH PLACE • THE JEWEL MERCHANTS • JOSEPH
HERGESHEIMER • THE JUDGING OF JURGEN • JURGEN • THE
KING WAS IN HIS COUNTING HOUSE • LADIES AND GENTLE-
MEN • LET ME LIE • THE LINEAGE OF LICHFIELD • THE LINE
OF LOVE • THE MUSIC FROM BEHIND THE MOON • THE
NIGHTMARE HAS TRIPLETS • PREFACE TO THE PAST • THE
RIVET IN GRANDFATHER'S NECK • THE SILVER STALLION •
SMIRE • SMIRT • SMITH • SOME OF US • SOMETHING ABOUT
EVE • SONNETS FROM ANTAN • SPECIAL DELIVERY • STRAWS
AND PRAYER-BOOKS • TABOO • THERE WERE TWO PIRATES •
THESE RESTLESS HEADS • TOWNSEND OF LICHFIELD • THE
WAY OF ECBEN • THE WHITE ROBE

COLLABORATIONS

BETWEEN DAWN AND SUNRISE (WITH JOHN MACY) • OF
ELLEN GLASGOW, AN INSCRIBED PORTRAIT (WITH ELLEN
GLASGOW) • THE ST. JOHNS (WITH A. J. HANNA)

GENEALOGIES

BRANCHIANA • BRANCH OF ABINGDON • THE MAJORS AND
THEIR MARRIAGES

LET ME LIE

*Being in the Main an Ethnological Account of
the Remarkable Commonwealth of Virginia
and the Making of Its History*

JAMES BRANCH CABELL

"Just take me back and let me lie . . .

in old Virginia."

1 9 4 7

Farrar, Straus and Company · New York

COPYRIGHT, 1947

BY JAMES BRANCH CABELL

818.5
C

MANUFACTURED IN THE U. S. A.
BY H. WOLFF, NEW YORK
DESIGNED BY STEFAN SALTER

To the treasured memory of
ELLEN GLASGOW

—not merely as having been without any peer among them who have adorned and commemorated the State of Virginia.

TABLE OF CONTENTS

An Editorial Note ൙

ABOUT MURDER
IN SELF-DEFENCE

SUNDRY portions of this ethnological treatise concerning the State of Virginia, it may be remarked, have been printed before today, in sundry periodicals, under the pen name of Branch Cabell. This was an abbreviation which I adopted in 1932 through motives of logic; and which, with the publication of *There Were Two Pirates*, I was led to put by, in some part by the advice of my publishers, but above all because of a selfish liking for personal comfort. Like any other not wholly irrational mammal, I have learned under the tuition of time to esteem comfort very far beyond logic. And so, when rearranging the contents of this monograph—during my at least comparative maturity in 1946—I have chosen to usurp all that which Branch Cabell contributed thereto.

My rather numerous reasons for decapitating in print, after 1930, the name under which the Biography of the Life of Manuel was completed during this year, at the unphilanthropic length of twenty-one allied books, have been recited upon two occasions—first, in *Townsend of Lichfield*, and later, in *These Restless Heads*. I wished, in brief, to distinguish between the Biography and anything which I might write afterward. The distinction as yet appears, to me at least, to have been rational, but to be rational, so I have found, does not of necessity beget comprehension, or prevent confusion.

I mean that, now for almost fifteen years, readers who chanced to be interested by some one or another of my books have been writing, sometimes to James Branch Cabell and at other times to Branch Cabell, upon the assumption that physically the two were different persons; our merits were compared, our divergences noted; and with a regrettable persistence was the question asked in what exact, if any, degree were the two of us related? Thereafter, when the letter was otherwise intelligent and friendly, I have had to appear uncivil by not answering it, or else I had to explain the entire matter, all over again.

I mean furthermore that a majority of these misled correspondents, under a pleasing delusion as to my local notoriety, have written to Branch Cabell, Richmond, Virginia. The "Deficiency in Address" then had to be supplied by the postal authorities of my native city, with an extremely soft pencil, and endorsed with a stamped notice of their research work—sometimes in red ink, but upon more impressive occasions in royal purple. After these labors had been concluded, my letters were delivered to Branch, Cabell & Company, a firm of Richmond stock brokers; and so in the course of business had to be opened and read, at least partially, by the employees of Branch, Cabell & Company before being relayed, for the second time, to me. I misrelish, apart from yet other considerations, thus to annoy the Post Office Department, as well as to put Branch, Cabell & Company to the recurrent postal expenses involved, so continually, and then all over again.

I mean too that, under my full name, I more than once have been introduced to affable creatures who had already met my kinsman Branch Cabell; and who in many cases knew him quite well. These statements I have made it a rule not ever to question; yet the situation tends toward awkwardness. It embarrasses me, who dislike argument, and who have come to dislike in particular having to argue about Branch Cabell, all over again.

Furthermore, I have had to encounter, with a depressing frequency, persons who ask me just why I did change my name. They are fairly pleasant about it; but the suspicion stays unhidden that in doing so I must have been up to no good; and it leads to a general feeling upon my part of speaking from the prisoner's dock throughout the none too brief while which I have to give up to making my reasons more or less clear, all over again.

Throughout fifteen years I have been thus troubled variously by the circumstance that in the eyes of the law, and in the teeth of what I thought to be rational, Branch Cabell and James Branch Cabell are condemned to remain the same author. In private, one may consider this to be a legal fiction; yet my nature is law-abiding; and in any case I have become very, very tired of attempting to explain their partial duality, all over again, thus endlessly.

For these and for yet other reasons of a right-mindedly selfish color, I have so nearly approached homicide as to abolish Branch Cabell; and in the Epilogue to this book he makes his final appearance.

JAMES BRANCH CABELL

Richmond-in-Virginia
12 October 1946

Acknowledgments 🦢

Grateful acknowledgment is made for permission to reproduce copyright material in LET ME LIE as follows:

"The Last Cry of Romance," *The Nation,* May 6, 1925. Reprinted by permission of *The Nation.*

"Two Sides of the Shielded," *Books,* April 20, 1930. Reprinted by permission of *Books.*

"Ellen Glasgow," *Book-of-the-Month Club News,* August, 1935. Reprinted by permission of the *Book-of-the-Month Club News.*

"Homage to Colonel Esmond, Late of Castlewood-in-Virginia," *Richmond News Leader,* September 8, 1937. Reprinted by permission of the *Richmond News Leader.*

"Messer Marco Polo, Sixteen Years Later," *Reading and Collecting,* October, 1937. Reprinted by permission of *Reading and Collecting.*

Of Ellen Glasgow, An Inscribed Portrait (preface by Ellen Glasgow), pamphlet. The Maverick Press, 1938. Reprinted by permission of the Maverick Press.

"Factual Fiction," *The Saturday Review of Literature,* April 11, 1942.

"The Arts in Gaza," *The Saturday Review of Literature,* August 1, 1942. Reprinted by permission of *The Saturday Review of Literature.*

Review of *A Certain Measure, New York Post* and *Chicago Sun,* December 2-5, 1943. Reprinted by permission of the *New York Post* and the *Chicago Sun.*

"A Letter to General Lee," *Atlantic Monthly,* March, 1946.

"Of Southern Ladies," *Atlantic Monthly,* May, 1946.

"Almost Touching the Confederacy," *Atlantic Monthly,* October, 1946. Reprinted by permission of the *Atlantic Monthly.*

"The Rivet in My Neck of Virginia," *Book News,* December, 1946. Reprinted by permission of *Book News.*

"Ellen Glasgow and the Legend of the 'Virginians,'" *Chicago Sun,* December 1, 1946. Reprinted by permission of the *Chicago Sun.*

"Mr. Dickens and Mr. Poe," *Vogue,* January 15, 1947. Reprinted by permission of *Vogue.*

The Prologue

QUIET ALONG THE POTOMAC

Let us take a drive through the Northern Neck of Virginia. It is a land rich in history and romance, charming in its hospitality, enchanting in its recreational facilities, inspiring in its scenic beauties. It is enticing and enthralling, for here are some of the finest bathing waters. It is historic and romantic, for here is the birthplace of makers of the American nation; here are the scenes of their courtships; here are the sacred memories of the mothers of statesmen. Washington himself called the Northern Neck "the garden of Virginia."

H. RAGLAND EUBANK

A Period Piece

1

Upon the Virginian side of the great river, it is a qualified quiet. It is parochial and illusive. It likewise is moribund. To me continually is every one of these traits made plain by the two radios which, for some morbid reason, or it may be through a kindly desire to aid the local electric light company, my wife patronizes intermittently, all day long, now that World War Number Two is preparing a millennium guaranteed to be free of any imperfection. Sandwiched between the pæans as to headache remedies and chewing gum and the rhapsodies over canned goods and cathartics, arrives hourly the caressing auricular massage of many "news commentators"; and they keep Poynton Lodge resonant with an epic of crushing defeats for the Axis Powers, annotated but now and then by a rumored trivial setback for the Allies, which, it is pleasing to hear, stays unconfirmed from any official source.

Yet my writing room stands at a fair distance from each radio; and time has touched charitably my ears, so that I need no longer hear very well. The soothing flood of misinformation thus reaches me in the more rational form of blurred chirps and squawks, and of occasional clucking noises, such as might be coming from out of a remote chicken run.

So I need to think hardly at all about World War Number Two during those hours in which I divert myself with writing. Outside the broad folding windows before me extends endlessly, so far as goes vision, the mouth of the Potomac, along with some half of Chesapeake Bay; and almost always a warship is passing there, sullenly, either to destroy or to be demolished. With an equal constantness, airplanes drone by only a little way above my head; and they penetrate the air of Northumberland County with the efficient and unhurried, buzzing, whirring pertinacity of an enlarged dentist's drill when they pass northward upon errands of state or return vice versa toward Langley Fields, near Norfolk, for overhauling.

Yet every one of these aids to demolition so far resembles that immeasurably more ruinous weapon of unreason, the radio, as to remain constantly perceptible without ever demanding the full attention of a resigned husband and taxpayer. I can ignore these, my own partial property, almost. I peep around the right-hand side of my reading glasses, it may be, toward the river, or else I inspect heaven, slantwise. I observe, in both quarters, my bucklers

4

against the Hun's hunger for homicide and Japan's unpraiseworthy addiction to all forms of atrocity.

I return then to more modest affairs. I resume my writing.

2

IT IS not, I protest (to myself at any rate), a mere weak-knee'd sort of escapism. I attend, rather, to my own business, which is the completing of a book. A book, I remind myself, may evoke pleasure; it may, at least possibly, turn out to be permanent; and either outcome is more than ever even the most ardent statesmen have asserted as to the special war they fomented.

Cheered by these inspiring reflections, I continue with my writing; and the war, that inconceivable huge horror, becomes only a slight, disregarded annoyance now that writing drugs me. I have lived through too many years to expect human beings to behave rationally; and the war, as yet, stays endurably remote, in its more violent aspects, from tiny Poynton Lodge and my adjacent sedate seven acres in the Northern Neck of Virginia.

3

THIS part of the state is called the Northern Neck because it is the northernmost of the four peninsulas, or "necks," into which, as in earth's first but no doubt inferior garden, four great rivers divide Tidewater Virginia. Southward, the York and the James flow under parvenu titles which stem from the seventeenth century. The Northern Neck adheres to antiquity; and thus drowses between the Quick-Rising-Water and the Stream of Swans—should you be so ill-advised as to translate into English the Indian names for the Rappahannock and the Potomac.

I cannot think these names are irrelevant. They indicate, to my judgment, so long after the last native Indian has quitted the Northern Neck, a spirit of conservatism which regards the English invasion of Virginia, in 1607, as an experiment such as may or may not be accepted—by-and-by, without any special need to hurry in one's decision—as a permanent arrangement. —For the Northern Neck avoids hurry; and it is, above all else, conservative. Its hazed pale atmosphere, indeed, has so very soothingly inoculated the English stock which came to this part of Virginia, about 1640, that few of the first settlers' descendants have left the peninsula of their own will. Not until 1927 did the people of the Northern

Neck so far yield to modernity as to permit a bridge over the Rappahannock; and thus condescended to associate almost intimately with the inferior and more impetuous parts of Virginia. As for Mr. Stephenson's mischancy invention, during 1829, of the locomotive steam engine, that flighty latter-day contraption has been so very severely ignored in our neighborhood that no railway has ever entered the Northern Neck.

Continuing to instruct you, I remark that this peninsula was once all one county, which in 1648 the English named Northumberland. Portions of it have been subdivided since then into Lancaster, and Westmoreland, and Richmond, and King George counties; and Old Northumberland contributed likewise to form a part of Stafford County; so that the present-day Northumberland is merely the northeastern tip of its former self.

When the English came, they found this peninsula to surpass every other section of the domains they were stealing upon the behalf of civilization; for here, in these fertile districts which the dispossessed Indians had called Ajacan and Chicacoan, were to be seen (it stays recorded) "many fine harbors. The water was deep near the shore, landlocked and sheltered, affording excellent anchorage. The lands adjacent to the rivers had been cleared and planted by the Indians, and all were in cultivation . . . The forests behind them afforded materials for building."

It followed that many of the more influential, and all the actively intelligent, of these English settlers applied for land grants in the Northern Neck because of its multiform advantages, which so very far outrivaled the sparse charms of settlements alongside the James and the York. The Northern Neck in this way became the home of Virginia's more opulent planters, who builded for their comfort's sake, not makeshift cabins, but mansions which, from the first, displayed amplitude and architectural flourishes of a baronial nature. The peninsula, in brief, was settled for the most part by persons of the upper classes who had the means to provide for themselves an especial and carefree sort of self-sufficiency such as does not any longer exist upon earth; for a large plantation, let it be remembered, alike produced and manufactured everything essential for its inhabitants, for its hundreds of inhabitants. It was a principality; and its national anthem, if it cared for such gauds, was borrowed from the Miller of Dee.

During this halcyon régime, it appears, we landholders did not even have to bother about money. One of these early Virginian planters, for example, reports, casually, to a correspondent in England:

"I have a large Family of my own, and my Doors are open to Every Body; yet I have no Bills to pay, and half a Crown will rest undisturbed in my Pocket for many Moons together. Like one of the Patriarchs, I have my Flocks and my Herds, my Bond-men and Bond-women, and every sort of Trade amongst my own Servants, so that I live in a kind of Independence on every one but Providence."

That an existence so untroubled does not appear credible to us, who are harried by a more enlightened civilization, one need not point out. Yet in all parts of the Northern Neck the gentry, once, thus flourished, and not any comfort did they lack, except, of course, plumbing. In this cosy, Old Testamental fashion, thrived hereabouts, everywhere between the Potomac and the Rappahannock, the Lees, the Eskridges, the Carters, the Mottrams, the Conways, the Fitzhughs, the Gascoignes, the Ayletts, the Coles, the Tayloes, and yet other pre-eminent clans. Many meritorious middle-class families, such as the Washingtons, and the Madisons (who indeed intermarried with the Conways), and the Monroes also, figured somewhat more modestly in the social scheme of the Northern Neck, and they produced presidents who, after their accession to office, were received with a patriotic and but slightly reserved affability by the very best people.

I pause here to think, with a flavor of human envy, about the liberal existence, deficient only as to bathrooms and water closets, which was granted throughout the course of some two centuries to the gentry of Virginia "before The War," as we phrase it hereabouts, because by the standards of all my neighbors there was never, not even today, but one really estimable war. It was fought between 1861 and 1865; and it ended the golden age of the great planters of the Northern Neck.

4

THEY were a gracious and kindly and a highly self-complacent race who had lived as princes, each with his own domain in the form of a plantation which provided its overlord, and his dozen or more legitimate children, and the two or three wives whom he used up in begetting these special children, with all the needs of life and with a fair number of life's luxuries. Of a sudden, in the April of 1865, these princelings became paupers. There was left only the plantation, which they had no means to cultivate, and the great mansion, which a retinue of servants alone could keep habitable. There were no more servants, now that the Negroes had been freed. There was no more money, now that Confederate money had become worthless. There was merely destitution.

To this destitution the unquelled gentry of the

Northern Neck of Virginia adapted themselves with the quiet good-breeding which befits the well-born in all circumstances. For the most part, they let the land go, perforce; so that nowadays their ancestral mansions gleam spickly and spanly after having been purchased, and lavishly plumbered and electrified, by magnates from out of the North. The offspring of the land's dispossessed peerage, far fallen from seigneury, have become truck farmers; or perhaps they conduct, casually, a fish boat, or a general merchandise store, or a filling station, or a soft drink stand, or a pharmacy, or it may be the village post office, with a complacent disregard for all rules of thrift and of system. They serve one another, in an unbusinesslike vein of friendship, as pastors or carpenters, or as physicians or plumbers, or as house painters; repayment remains optional; and they earn in this way, somehow, a haphazard but untroubled livelihood without ever having to leave the Northern Neck, which has fixed upon them its pallid enchantment.

—Pallid, because in this strip of land between two huge rivers the air tends always toward haziness, so that (in the present Northumberland, at any rate) from April onward a fair way into November, the weather stays ever autumnal. 'Twas a phenomenon observed gratefully by my former neighbor, Colonel Henry Esmond of Castlewood (over in Westmoreland County), who has noted down, in his Memoirs, how unfailingly "on the beautiful banks of the Potomac . . . we have a season, the calmest and the most delightful of the year, which we call the Indian summer."

One is thus able, for all practical ends, to inhabit a kind of permanent September until winter arrives —a sharp, brutal, but brief winter, during which you remain indoors so as to mend drowsily your fishnets, or to play checkers, or to read through, completely, the two mail-order catalogues, beside an upright, round red-hot stove, with a tomato can, half-full of rusty brown water, seething on top of it. —For during the winter one becomes ursine and hibernates. One awaits, in a contented torpor, the sudden bright coming of April, which through a pardonable Hibernianism arrives as the rule during March, on or about St. Patrick's Day.

5

THROUGHOUT the stay of this eight-months-long autumn, the surprisingly fertile soil of Northumberland produces all needed fruits and grains and vegetables upon a minimum provocation of farming. A volunteer posse of bee martins defends your plowed lands from the thieving crow. Your swine repay lavishly that slight healthful exercise which has disposed of your garbage by emptying it into their troughs. Turkeys and poultry and horses and cattle attend virtually to their own sustenance. Toward autumn, as the calendar counts autumn, rabbits appear to contend during the night season for the honor of being the first rabbit to enter your traps. Alongside the Potomac, all nature of fish and of hard-shell crabs require merely to be released from your nets and crab pots, while soft crabs await flaccidly their doom, to be lifted with a hand-net, from out of your private "back creek," into the kitchen.

I concede that partridges and quail and squirrel do demand of an epicure the exertion of hunting them before they consent to become viands; yet almost every acre of Northumberland affords all three; and with this slight churlish exception, food seems to provide itself.

That your not in the least bit baronial home is snug and exceedingly well designed for your needs is ensured by the fact that you yourself builded it, with the neighbors aiding companionably. Clothing is not a problem. You will not be judged by your clothing, in a community which knows quite as much about you (as well as about your parents and your grand-parents) as you yourself know; in which most of your feminine elders have been at pains, time and again, to change your diapers; and which, in short, is composed well-nigh entirely of your more or less near relatives. The people of the Northern Neck, after three centuries of intermarriage, live wholly, as it were, *en famille*.

In common with your begetters—those genial, arrogant bewigged burgesses and county lieutenants and members of the Governor's Council—you do not have any money to speak of; but, then, neither does anybody else. And moreover, did you possess (as in our neighborhood a strangely cryptic phrase defines opulence) money to roll in, there still would not be in Northumberland County any luxuries for you to purchase. In order to spend your money, you would be put to the annoyance of riding upon the Greyhound Bus all the long ninety miles to Richmond— and this is an excursion into pagan regions such as is made by no sane Northumberlander except for the purpose of being operated upon for appendicitis.

6

To LIVE in the Northern Neck, in brief, is a transaction so very full of letting well enough alone that one cannot but wonder how, for so many years, this uncivilized practice has escaped correction. That in due course a more seemly form of Americanism will root out our backward and shiftless contentment, there is no doubting; already the battleships of international brotherhood are within eyereach; the airplanes of altruism toil overhead well laden with destructiveness; and imbecility's main aide, the radio, enables more and yet more often the high sentiments of our leading statesmen to invade the clean air of Northumberland. All portents proclaim that the ancient, the irrational, and the wholly comfortable complacence of the Northern Neck of Virginia is, as I remarked earlier, moribund.

Even so, our foredoomed Indian summer is not yet ended, not utterly. I get out of its indolence a pleasure which appears doubly dear on account of my knowledge that everything hereabouts is now perishing, surely and so speedily that, at any instant, the very last bit of it, including me, is likely to be demolished. All faiths and all customs and all codes are being smashed up—with a Miltonic garnish of dust and heat—throughout all our planet. Here is quiet; and an obsolete sort of sanity; and a familiar, if rather shabby and slipshod, comfort; nor as yet have efficiency and desolation, or even any special virulence of mankind's more noble motives, entered into the Northern Neck of Virginia.

Such invaders will come in due course. Meanwhile, I am mildly pleased by the progress of the book in hand; my modest farmlands flourish under a season of notably fine weather; and I can look back with contentment upon a fair number of years of living without dishonor in a world which, by and large, I have found to be both pleasant and interesting. There is still a little money in bank, overlooked by the Collector of Internal Revenue; my wife and son, and our dog also, are so well suited to my taste that I would not care to see any one of the three in any manner improved; and Poynton Lodge likewise, in its unpretentious way, contents me well enough. There is no possible mansion in the sky for which I incline to barter Poynton Lodge, not immediately.

7

MEANWHILE, somewhere outside the serene and as yet untroubled Northern Neck, a war is in progress, and several thousand champions of the American way of living are at loggerheads pretty much everywhere. They are fighting near Livorno in Italy, upon Saipan Island in the South Pacific, at La Haye de Puits in Normandy, at Mitkyina in Burma, and alongside the Siang-kiang in China, as well as at a great number of other places with the pronunciation of which all "news commentators" are fighting but a very little less bravely.

A fair number of us stay-at-homes, at this instant, have no precise notion as to the aims of World War

Number Two, beyond the "unconditional surrender" of Germany and Japan; after which, it is agreed generally, all the more noble ideals which, upon this warm Sunday morning, are inciting everybody can be determined on at leisure, and our planet will become a superior paradise.

Pending this desirable outcome, a majority of my neighbors, at the moment I commemorate, are talking about the more convenient illegal channels through which to obtain automobile tires and gasoline and undiluted whiskey; about those strange new Robot bombs which for the last three weeks have been troubling England; and about the spectacular burning of the main tent of the Ringling Brothers and Barnum & Bailey Circus, at Hartford in Connecticut, last Thursday.

8

TOWARD no one of these pre-eminent topics of my era do I feel incited to direct an intelligent and broad-minded concern. I reflect, instead, that the dauntless attempts of our armies and of our navies to smash the Axis would seem to have aroused among my fellow-civilians a similar intrepidity with which to rebuff reason.

I observe, for example, that the *Richmond Times-Dispatch* repudiates all unsavory rumors as to the young women who are now serving their country as WACs or as WAVEs. The fact that "their spiritual life has nowhere been neglected" is demonstrated conclusively by reproducing "a view of Lieutenant Flora Flaherty, WAC, kneeling before the altar in St. Paul's Church, as specially posed for our Staff Photographer."

With a logic no less forthright and uplifting does the *Richmond News-Leader* reply to a lately enlisted seaman, newly turned eighteen, who before going abroad to preserve the American way of living desires, blushingly, to learn if a marriage in which the husband was younger than the wife could be thought sensible. The *News-Leader* assures him that many successful and famous persons, such as Napoleon Bonaparte and William Shakespeare and Clark Gable, have all married women who were older than themselves.

In Virginia's capital city the circumstance is now recognized that "a protection for any son or husband in active service" is the gift of a conveniently small Bible in steel covers. This, when worn in the left-hand breast pocket, can be relied on both to attract and to deflect all bullets. Each of the aforementioned Richmond papers advertises reverently such Bibles; and the leading Richmond department store reports a sale of more than eleven hundred copies during the last month.

Congress has been called upon to sustain the morale of our troops by providing free beauty-parlor treatment, with face-lifting included, for the legal wives of all soldiers, airmen, and sailors whom the Selective Service Act has privileged to uphold the American way of living abroad in a uniform. This philanthropic measure is being hailed with widespread approval, throughout the entire Northern Neck, now that the Fifth War Loan Drive has been ended, at four o'clock yesterday afternoon, with a fair margin of oversubscribing.

"—For the government has got a plenty of money," so do we put it comprehensively; "and the boys ought to have a nice-looking wife to come home to. It will be the very best thing in the world for them."

9

WHAT though am I, reflection reminds me, to fret over the fact that *Homo sapiens* does not often display sapiency? and of what worth were the prolonged years of writing if my fellow-creatures should elect to stultify every one of my books by behaving with intelligence? With an entire planet in arms to justify Poictesme's blunt motto, *Mundus Vult Decipi*, I ought to be wholly pleased.

"*Carpe diem*," I remark, in my most polished

scholastic manner, during the same instant that I feed into my typewriter a fresh sheet of paper.

—For the day, as yet, remains dulcet. To my right hand I observe with approval an entangled and lazy undulation of mimosa foliage, made vivid at this special moment with its gray-and-pink, thistle-like flowering. Three hummingbirds have poised there, like pulsing jewels. To my left hand a grotesquely out-of-date, tall whatnot flaunts, in porcelain, its symbolically fragile medley of reptiles and of fish and of water fowl. All these, I reflect, are the toys of a time-battered child; and, as yet, I take pleasure in them. Before me extends, endlessly, the hazed skyline of the quiet and now greenish-blue Potomac, which at the instant no part of our navy animates. I have heard not one airplane since lunch; and my lunch, an excellent lunch, of earth's very best asparagus and soft crabs and full-bodied Northumberland butter and cool sliced bread, is being digested all-placidly.

Nothing troubles me at this moment except only my knowledge of its impermanence. The one world which I ever knew or cared about is now demolishing itself upon loud moral principles; and my one certainty as concerns the future is that I shall not very much like it. Meanwhile, perched here precariously and playing futilely with a typewriter and a schoolboy's Examination Pad, while Armageddon blusters and perjures and annihilates, I am allowed at worst to savor some final half-seconds of contentment in the uncivilized Northern Neck.

—Wherewith I resume my writing: for at a moment so momentous it does not seem wholesome to leave undischarged any part of a duty unquietable and resistless, now that I too have set about the task which is laid upon every native Virginian author; and have started to put together a book of homage to the remarkable Commonwealth of Virginia.

Part One ⮂

THE FIRST VIRGINIAN

Virginia, thy Golden Age is yet to be. Giants hadst thou in the days of old, but thy race of giants is not yet dead. Into the footsteps of the fathers the feet of a new generation are treading with sturdy yet reverent steps. The winter of thy discontent is over and the new blood of a vernal season is within thy breast. It is coursing through the veins of thy mountains. 'Tis running in thy streams down hillsides. 'Tis singing in thy rivers that run to the sea. Venerated Mother of States! thou art moving in the march of progress.

RABBI EDWARD N. CALISCH

1

THAT the earliest known Virginian should have changed completely the history of the present United States of America was that which Virginia expects of all her children, upon the birthdays of her more notable deceased heroes, and at college commencements, and upon yet other instructive occasions when orators roam unleashed. Equally as a matter of course was he a by-product of the Northern Neck—that unparalleled locality which (even by an historian no less leading than our own Virginian, H. Ragland Eubank) has been termed "The Birthplace of Genius" as well as "The Land of the Giants."

I am not certain, however, that the modesty with which Virginia has failed to dwell upon the exploits, or at all freely to concede the existence, of her first famous son, is quite equally of course a by-product of Virginia's dislike for any nature of boastfulness.

It has been unsettling to maternal pride, perhaps, to find the son older than the mother; and the first native Virginian to figure in history became known to Europeans a good forty-odd years before Virginia was founded—when in 1560, or by another account in 1559, a party of Spanish explorers returned into the harbor of Vera Cruz bringing with them the Prince of Ajacan. These Spaniards, in Spain's perennial search for a water route across North America toward Japan and India, had entered Chesapeake Bay, and they sailed some slight distance up the Potomac under the belief that the broad Stream of Swans also was an arm of the ocean. When the fact became noticeable that their caravel, instead, was ascending a river, they landed upon its south bank, in the present Northern Neck of Virginia.

Hereabouts then lived Ajacan Indians; and these pagans acclaimed the coming of the Spaniards with a hospitality such as all Christian peoples recommend when abroad, entertaining the white men for some two or three weeks. When the explorers made ready to leave, a young chieftain of the Ajacans wished to go with them so that he might become familiar with Christian customs; and his praiseworthy desire was gratified.

In this fashion did the first known of all native Virginians get to Mexico; and there the conversion to Christianity of the Prince of Ajacan was hailed as an affair of considerable importance, both pious and political. We do not know, with certainty, the Indian name of the first Virginian: it is reported to have been Nemattanon; but we do know that when the Indian Prince was baptized, with a befitting pomp, in the Cathedral of the City of Mexico, the

Viceroy of New Spain served as godfather and gave
to the pre-eminent refugee from pagan error his
own name: so that henceforward the first Virginian
about whom anybody knows anything was called
Luis de Velasco.

2

FOR the next ten years he moves, variously and un-
restingly, in a glittering cloud, as it were, of hear-
say such as appears to have bewildered the judgment of his associates. You must remember that to
the Spaniards he figured as the overlord of an un-
imaginable and magic-haunted realm in the vast
fairyland which was North America; all wonders
were possible there; and besides that, even the first
Virginian, when it came to talking about his birthplace, was a liar of considerable magnitude. "His
representations of the prosperous and cultural conditions of his people were highly colored," is the
staid fashion in which one historian, Dr. Michael
Kenny, has indicated this racial trait.

According to yet another record, "the Indian
Prince . . . spoke, without vainglory, as to the
twenty noble cities and the seventy-two main towns
of Ajacan, no one of which, as the Prince admitted,
was builded wholly of gold, because after due trial
his people had found a uniformly metallic architec-
ture to become monotonous. Their buildings, for

this reason, were very much varied with sardonyx
and ivory and crystal and jasper . . . In reply to
further questions, his Highness described Ajacan as
a fairly extensive kingdom, but denied its being far
more than double the size of Europe, if one included
Russia."

Such accuracy was impressive. Don Luis thus convinced all his hearers that the present Northern
Neck of Virginia was an opulent, vast, pagan earthly
paradise which, under the influence of his diplo-
macy, might by-and-by be persuaded—it stayed
possible—to form an alliance with Spain. The live-
liness of his fancy, yet furthermore, connected the
headwaters of the Potomac River with the Pacific
Ocean; and afforded benignantly to his Spanish
friends, in this way, the long sought-for short water
route toward Asia.

So we soon find the Prince near Madrid, in the
King's private chamber at the Escorial, lying with
the customary fervor of an American statesman, but
with an unusual convincingness, to King Philip II
about Ajacan. The King was enchanted. As Wood-
bury Lowery has summed up this episode, "On his
arrival at Court, Don Luis, who was intelligent and
of an agreeable address, ingratiated himself to such
an extent into the good-will of Philip II that he lived
at the royal expense during all his stay." Moreover,
the King granted to his cousin of Ajacan the rank

of a grandee of Spain with a pension befitting that high estate; whereafter the first Virginian prospered as a well-to-do nobleman, in and about the most splendid court in Europe.

He was admired as a bright paragon of civilized culture, now that his scholarship had become considerable; his affability charmed everyone; and his indiscretions, even in the best bedrooms, stayed cloaked with a tact worthy of a bishop; for—yet again to quote from an historian of the first rank— "in all forms of Christian conduct and practice Don Luis de Velasco appears to have been exemplary."

He fared thus for an easeful, glittering, and forever affable decade, throughout every moment of which, in various portions of Spain's then enormous empire, the industry of his imagination was requited with opulence and applause. Some part of this time he spent in Havana; and when he went from Cuba into Florida, during the same year that Pedro Menéndez invaded the peninsula, he is reported to have shared in the founding of St. Augustine, during the September of 1565. It is certain that Don Luis passed the winter of 1565-66 at St. Augustine, as the friend and confidant of Menéndez.

All this is a matter of history, which was recorded by Solís de Merás, as Menéndez' biographer and brother-in-law (who applauds especially Don Luis' intelligence and sound Christian principles), and by

still other Spanish historians of the late sixteenth
century.

It is equally a matter of history that, through the
efforts of Menéndez, the first known Virginian was
sent back into the Northern Neck of Virginia, in the
autumn of 1570, at the head of a Spanish colony
consisting of two priests, three brothers and three
scholastics of the Society of Jesus, as well as four
attendants. By the plan of Menéndez, these staunch
churchmen during the winter months, under God's
protection and the protection of Don Luis de Velasco,
"would subdue the fierce hearts of the native Indians to the mild tenets of Christianity." Then, when
spring returned, Menéndez would come with
enough soldiers and firearms to take care of their
bodies, and to put ashore new settlers.

The lively but pious Prince, who to be sure was
offered no choice in the matter, accepted this mission with every seeming of joy, now that he was
privileged to go back into his native land (in the
words of his fond admirer, Brother Juan Carrera,
of the Society of Jesus) "as a Paul of the Holy Faith
. . . burning with zeal . . . to carry the Gospel to
Ajacan."

3

His expedition reached Don Luis' former home, at
the mouth of the Potomac, safely; and turning to

the left, ascended one of the river's tributaries for a distance of several miles before disembarking, "in midstream." This lengthy and broad and shallow tributary, beyond any reasonable doubt, must have been the Coan River; so that the Jesuits, I infer, landed in small row boats not far from the present Heathsville, in what is now Northumberland County, where the caravel left them in the all-capable hands of Don Luis de Velasco, and returned toward Mexico.

By his fellow-tribesmen Don Luis was received with delight, "as one re-arisen from the dead," and his Spanish friends were greeted with politeness. All Ajacan, after hearing Don Luis' advice, thronged gladly toward Christian instruction. The Jesuits, for their greater comfort, now that winter approached, were removed yet further up the Coan River, and then overland to the shores of the Rappahannock. There (not very far from the village called Sharps, it has been estimated) the Indians aided their spiritual fathers in building a trim chapel, so that all offices of the Catholic Church might be conducted suitably.

Never had anyone witnessed in the Northern Neck a more devout autumn. The Ajacans were converted by scores and hundreds. Only when winter had closed in, and when there remained no chance of a Spanish ship's reaching Ajacan until late in the following spring, did Don Luis command his people to scalp and disembowel the white men. The remnants were buried courteously before Don Luis set fire to the chapel.

4

IT FOLLOWED that when, in the spring of 1571, the Spaniards sent provisions and reinforcements for the first white colony to be established in the present State of Virginia, they could not find any trace of the Jesuits, or of Don Luis either, because he had withdrawn his people from out of the Northern Neck, going up into the Blue Ridge Mountains, it is said, beyond reach of the Spaniards' anger. Inasmuch as Spain's sole guarantee for the success of the proposed colony had been the good offices of this debonair, but now missing, "Paul of the Holy Faith," the new colonists did not land; and after hanging the few available Indians, Menéndez sailed southward. Spain had given up the notion of settling that territory which is now Virginia; and did not ever renew the attempt after this decisive setback.

Don Luis de Velasco so vanishes from out of human knowledge, and not anything more is recorded, with any certainty, about the first of all Virginians who entered history.

5

To DECLARE this massacre beside the Rappahannock River an important event is to deal in the brusque and brittle art of understatement a bit over-profusely. But for Don Luis de Velasco, the Spanish reinforcements would have landed unopposed in the spring of 1571, and yet further military forces and more settlers would have followed them during the summer, as was foreplanned. In a situation so far more favorable for a colony than was any other part of the present Virginia, there seems no apparent reason why a Spanish settlement should not have thrived and extended, under the continued favor of Don Luis de Velasco. The present-day Commonwealth of Virginia, and in due course the entire Atlantic seaboard between the Potomac and Florida, would have become a Spanish province; nor would Jamestown ever have been heard of.

I do not deal in fancy but in logic. The Carolinas and Georgia could not conceivably have been occupied by the English when once Spanish military posts had been established to the north and the south of this area. The one claim to this territory, indeed, which the English ever advanced for themselves was based upon a contention that Spain's failure to colonize Spain's lands anywhere north of Florida had caused Spain to forfeit these lands to the first comer.

And the first comer, as appears usual in such cases, was British; for about twelve years after the Rappahannock massacre, England's devout queen, Elizabeth Tudor, grieved to observe that these "heathen and barbarous lands" remained "not actually possessed of any Christian prince or people"; and she, in consequence, granted to Sir Walter Raleigh, as her court's leading atheist, a charter to occupy all such "countreys and territories," for the good of their inhabitants' souls' health. In this manner began the Colony of Virginia.

It follows, I submit, that the Indian-born Don Luis de Velasco changed, and in changing he predetermined, the fate of a continent. He left it free to become English; and but for his intervention no one of the South Atlantic states would, or indeed could, have been settled by British pioneers. No other native Virginian has ever achieved—unintentionally, it is true—an action of so tremendous significance.

Nor, I imagine, would any state except Virginia have ignored resolutely the entire performance because it did not involve persons of Teutonic ancestry. No Anglo-Saxons were present at this massacre; and so, to us proud cousins of the Hun, what did this massacre matter?

6

INASMUCH as the first historians to write about Don Luis de Velasco were sound Catholics, they explained the killing of the defenceless Jesuits upon the sonorous if indefinite ground that, after his return into the Northern Neck, Don Luis "reverted to savagery." And that explanation, I protest, is plain balderdash. The man had lived, for some ten years, among the most widely enlightened persons of the prime of the Elizabethan age. The influence of a decade, and far more of a decade so all-glorious and so stimulating mentally, does not vanish overnight.

Don Luis, it must be remembered, had become very thoroughly and variously cultured; far more completely than the provincial and simple-hearted Jesuits, his victims, did he embody the higher civilization of Europe; and besides (it is needful to recall), in order to retain for himself affluence and applause and every other agreeability of life, he had merely to do nothing. With the colony once established, he was free to return, as a benefactor of all Spain, toward the amenities of his handsome estate in Europe; and as a benefactor of the Catholic Church, he was assured of an equally friendly reception in heaven whensoever he needed to ask for it.

He chose, instead, to become the first patriot in our history. He had lived in Mexico, he had lived in

Cuba, he had lived in Florida; and he unavoidably had observed, in all these colonies, what happened to the native Indians when once the white man had got a foothold among them. It followed that after patiently awaiting, throughout the course of five months, for the most advantageous moment, he destroyed the white men who had invaded his country, and he withdrew his people beyond reach of the white men.

As to the morality of his conduct there may be question; for the virtue of patriotism when it is displayed by the wrong nation becomes, as we all know, an atrocity. There can be no question whatever that Don Luis de Velasco acted with complete wisdom so far as went the welfare of his own people. He preserved his people from being despoiled and decimated and enslaved; and in order to secure this end he sacrificed himself. No other explanation is possible, I submit, for the behavior of this once preeminent Catholic and grandee of Spain after his enforced return into the Northern Neck.

7

HERE I have dwelled only upon the decisive part which was played by Don Luis de Velasco in the history of the yet unborn United States of America, without trying to be specific in aught else which concerns him. I have been thus specific in other pages, in as many indeed as 309 pages.

My point here is merely that this first Virginian patriot, to whom all Virginia owes its existence, may be encountered in an incalculable number of histories which deal with Spain's rôle in the settlement of North America or with the beginnings of the Catholic Church in this hemisphere. He figures in the history of Florida and of Mexico. But you will not find a full account, or it may be even a mention, of Don Luis de Velasco in any orthodox history of Virginia.

We prefer to begin our history in 1607, with the founding of Jamestown by Captain John Smith, who, if perhaps an almost appreciably less talented liar than Don Luis de Velasco, was at any rate Anglo-Saxon; and who ought not to be deprived of his just glory as the founder of Jamestown, we feel, by the subordinate fact that (since he then lay in fetters on shipboard under a charge of mutiny) he did not have any part in the founding of Jamestown. So does it follow that from the somewhat rigorously exclusive history of Virginia—which, like all other praiseworthy histories known to mankind, has been compiled by prejudice and edited by fancy—we omit, and we shall continue (I imagine) to omit forever, the first Virginian.

It is true that beside the wall of the "restored" Catholic Cemetery at Aquia, in remote Stafford County, one finds a bronze tablet "inscribed to the memory of the heroic Jesuit missionaries who, coming from Spain to bring Christ's gospel to the Indians in this Aquia region, erected near by in 1570, A. D., the first Christian temple in our northern land, Our Lady of Ajacan, and, expressly because of their Christian teachings, were by the natives treacherously slain."

Nor would it, I admit, appear seemly to find fault with the precision of a tablet "erected by the Catholic Students' Mission Crusade and their friends of the Diocese of Richmond," beyond noting that the eight Spaniards happen not to have been killed "expressly because of their Christian teachings" (which nobody in Ajacan regarded seriously), but as the advance guard of an army of occupation; as well as that to describe a chapel builded in the present Richmond County upon the north bank of the Rappahannock River as being "in this Aquia region," and "near by," exhibits very much the same beguiling light-mindedness as to geography which graced Don Luis de Velasco's own accounts of his country.

Such minor flaws one is quick to dismiss, in view of the circumstance that as a sample of Virginiana this tablet is more than sound. It is characteristic. It commemorates not what did happen but what ought to have happened.

—For near Aquia was established the second Catholic colony in Virginia, about the year 1650; and nothing could be more suitable than to have it founded, and made permanent, upon the same spot where the first Catholic settlers perished in 1571. The event would be poetic justice flavored with a discreet hint of the miraculous. So the incivic negligence of Don Luis de Velasco, in tomahawking the eight Jesuits elsewhere, has been rectified officially by means of this tablet; and we have expressed our disapproval of his lack of forethought yet furthermore by seeing to it that upon this tablet he remains unmentioned. He, after all, was not Anglo-Saxon.

8

TACTLESSLY, I once compiled an account of the life and exploits of Don Luis de Velasco. No more than any other known biography was the completed work in its every paragraph an exact record of unarguably established facts; as in any other biography, its writer had found gaps which needed to be bridged in a twilight of probability, with the aid of guesswork —as when, for example, I assumed Menéndez to have been the unknown explorer who first brought

Don Luis into Mexico. But at no point where the facts about Don Luis de Velasco remained attested were these facts violated. My authorities for these facts were cited, in a duly impressive-looking, rather closely printed bibliography, five pages long; and this staid tome, this scholastic parergon, was published, in the January of 1942, as *The First Gentleman of America*. It was received, you must let me boast, with mild favor.

Which was pleasant. And yet, what frame of mind, I was soon wondering, befits the plodding historian when the result of his patient and pedestrian labors is acclaimed as a not unsatisfying romance? If readers like the book—reflection whispers—what more can a sane author require? And should his reviewers upon the whole commend it as desirable reading-matter, why, then, what livelier form of Rhadamanthine charity can a reviewer be hoped to exhibit? The historian in such circumstances has not (I admitted) any personal grievance; for the injustice involved does not hurt him or his prosperity; but works, rather, to exaggerate his inventiveness and to augment his income.

Nevertheless did my conscience trouble me— though but never so civilly and with a refraining from violence such as bespoke its long years of well-bred coercion—over the reception granted to *The First Gentleman of America*. People at large, and in print also, were quite affable as to "this fantasy," or as some phrased it, "this ironic romance," which commemorated "the legendary adventures of a prince of a mythic country." The fact that the adventures were no more legendary than the country was mythic stayed untouched and ignored: for it was not possible (said common-sense) that any events so important could have occurred in Virginia without getting into the official history of Virginia.

So no one of my upon the whole kindly critics believed that this Nemattanon, who became Don Luis de Velasco, had ever existed; his Ajacan (which, as I have said, along with Chicacoan, once formed the Northern Neck of Virginia) was ranked as a province of Poictesme; my bibliography was dismissed with a shrug as mere harmless fooling; and the circumstance that I duly listed some dozens of widely honored historians who had preceded me in narrating the tale of Luis de Velasco was accepted, with a benign indulgence, as a fair sample of my ingenuity in inventing historians.

Since a half-dozen or so of them still live, and are known to me as persons, that in a way was embarrassing: for the professorial, with never so many collegiate honors and doctorates and a fair segment of *Who's Who in America* to their credit, do not relish, I found, being referred to jocosely as fictitious characters evolved by an irresponsible fancy to serve as adjuncts to an "ironic romance."

It was to no purpose that, in the columns of the *Saturday Review of Literature*, I admitted my theft from veracity of the entire story; nor did it at all matter that in even more stately quarters the book was estimated, by such authentic authorities concerning Virginian records as are Virginius Dabney and Douglas Freeman and Clayton Torrence, in the light of its exposition of history. To these scholars the origin of my story was familiar enough; but to the reading public in general *The First Gentleman of America* remained, as it still remains, "the legendary adventures of the prince of a mythic country."

Nothing whatever can be done about it, of course, so long as we Virginians continue to edit the official history of our state, as Ellen Glasgow has put it, "in the more freely interpretative form of fiction," and at the dictates of personal taste. Nor may I complain: for to be accredited with an imagination so lively as to have made up the entire incredible tale of Don Luis de Velasco is flattering. Yet I would have preferred, even at the cost of some undeserved plaudits, to convince my fellow-Virginians that in the history of our nation's making, the first chapter was contributed by a Virginian whom they have snubbed and forgotten.

Part Two &

MYTHS OF THE OLD DOMINION

This sacred spot [Jamestown Island] is hallowed with priceless memories. The very air we breathe is fragrant with the incense of offerings laid upon the altars of liberty and constitutional government. Here was made the first permanent settlement of the English race on this continent. Here success crowned the first armed resistance to British tyranny, and hurled from his palace, which stood upon this spot, a royal hireling. With loving and devoted hands the women of this country have saved from the ravages of the flood this birthplace of the greatest nation the sun ever shone upon.

JAMES ALSTON CABELL

1

*The scene is the Red Drawing Room of Poynton
Lodge, in Northumberland County, Virginia; and
Dr. Alonzo Juan Hernandez, that noted authority
upon Floridian history, has but now resumed a con-
versation momentarily disturbed by the need of
preparing two beverages.*

HERNANDEZ:——For indeed, when you tell me that
you consider it troubling to the convictions of a Virginian to study as you have done, in some slight degree, the history of Florida, I can perceive your
meaning, without granting for one instant that any
power in nature can upset the faith of a native Virginian as to the myths among which he was reared.
Even so, it pleases me to find a living Virginian who
admits that Florida has any history at all.

CABELL: You become ardent. Do you not need a
trifle more ice?

HERNANDEZ: I thank you; and so must any other
Floridian become ardent when he considers the pre-
tensions which have been advanced for Virginia,
over and yet over again, and in the teeth of all evidence, at the expense of Florida. ——For it was in
Florida, as we both well know, that the civilization
of the white man had its beginning in the present

United States of America. In Florida this civilization has persisted continuously since 1564. I have yet to find the Virginian who can either deny this fact or concede it with candor. You speak merely of Jamestown.

CABELL: You mistake matters. We of Virginia do not deny that in Florida the Spaniards held precariously an obscure outpost, of some sort or another, more or less prior to 1607, when at Jamestown was founded the first permanent English settlement, and when our nation began there. Yet inasmuch as these Spaniards (perhaps through no fault of their own, as we concede handsomely) were not Anglo-Saxon—

HERNANDEZ: There is not at Jamestown any settlement, nor for many decades has the forlorn island been inhabited except by mosquitoes and a caretaker. Jamestown is a mere mob of monuments and memorial tablets. The more charitable might admire Jamestown as a cemetery pleasingly deficient in corpses; but most certainly no one could call it a settlement. How then may we term "permanent" that which does not exist?

CABELL: Yes; but the descendants of the colonists—

HERNANDEZ: Now, St. Augustine has existed ever since the September of 1565, when Pedro Menéndez de Avilés founded this as yet thriving city—a fair generation's length before the English had intruded into lands which then were legally the north portion of Florida, and upon which they builded their transient Jamestown. And this much, as I need hardly remind you, applies equally to Sir Walter Raleigh's Lost Colony, which during the 1580's endured briefly in that other part of Florida which nowadays is called North Carolina.

CABELL: You indulge in hair-splitting. From the moment that those lands, which effete Spain claimed, on account of having owned them for but little more than a century, were occupied and christened Virginia by sturdy Anglo-Saxons, Virginia did exist; and the romantic history of Virginia began, in the April of 1607—

HERNANDEZ: Even by your own definition, the romantic history of Virginia must have begun in 1585, when those Spanish lands which today compose the State of North Carolina were occupied and christened Virginia by a band of English adventurers such as you prefer to call "sturdy Anglo-Saxons"; and as a yet further consequence, North Carolina must, in reality, be Virginia.

CABELL: But not at all. It is merely that in 1585 the first attempt to settle the Colony of Virginia was made at Roanoke Island in North Carolina, for indeed in this special part of Virginia was the birthplace of the colony's first daughter, Virginia Dare—

HERNANDEZ: One does not instantly perceive how the fact that Virginia Dare was born in 1587 within the present State of North Carolina could have caused the present State of Virginia to become her birthplace twenty years later.

CABELL: She was born, you must let me remind you, in what was then called "Virginia," and in lands which, a while afterward, were occupied and held for some time by the Colony of Virginia—

HERNANDEZ: To assert that because of this fact she ought to rank as a Virginian is a course of logic by which Kosciusko must be called Russian; by which Molière and Ibsen would become Germans; and by which all the Pharaohs would be turned into Englishmen. Indeed, now that you speak of the nonsense which you Virginians talk as to the first American-born white child—

CABELL: I did not speak of it.

HERNANDEZ: Not today, perhaps; but I am certain that at one time or another you must have done so, inasmuch as there is no Virginian who does not indulge in this nonsense. And it puzzles me thus to observe the unreason with which you struggle to deprive North Carolina of a distinction which, beyond any question, belongs to Florida. It is a matter of record that a considerable if undetermined number of white children had been born in Florida, at the French colony called Fort Caroline, prior to the

September of 1565, when Menéndez captured this citadel, inasmuch as he reported officially, even to the King of Spain, that among these children were "eight or ten boys" without troubling to count the girls.

CABELL: Yes; but—

HERNANDEZ: During the following year, in 1566, St. Augustine became the birthplace of Martin de Arguëlles, the first American-born white inhabitant of the present United States whose name has been preserved. After that, some score of white children were born at St. Augustine before Virginia Dare had been added to the population of North America. Prior to her birth, several white children born in Florida had begotten their own children. White children were as much a matter of course as scrub palmettoes in and about Florida when North Carolina produced Virginia Dare.

CABELL: They were white children, that is true; but no one of them was Anglo-Saxon.

HERNANDEZ: I am answered; for before the fond pride with which Virginians of the old school describe themselves as being "Anglo-Saxon," even in the same instant that they claim descent from the best Norman-French families, and speak complacently as to their Scotch-Irish grandparents, logic remains dumb. Yet pride cannot alter geography. Pride cannot remove Roanoke Island from

49

the eastern coast of Dare County, in North Carolina, into the confines of Virginia; and so, when you Virginians begin to speak of this perennial Dare infant as being the first child to be born in "the Colony of Virginia," I find it expedient to reflect that her father was called Ananias.

CABELL: The coincidence of the Christian name of Master Ananias Dare is not of necessity an apologue.

HERNANDEZ: One might question that, in view of the disregard for all forms of truthfulness which was shown by those whom you call "sturdy Anglo-Saxons" after they had become entrenched at Jamestown.

CABELL: It is possible, I confess, for the cynic to weigh with shrugs those high moral principles on account of which the English immigrants were forced to steal tract after tract of Spanish territory, in order to extend their civilization southward, through both of the Carolinas, and then through Georgia. That in this continuous land-grabbing the English were prompted always by the most lofty motives, they themselves have admitted; and yet perhaps, to the inconsiderate, the continued robberies which were dictated by philanthropy, and endorsed by the Anglican Church, might seem to reduce the all-glorious founding of Jamestown to the first larceny in a prolonged and successful career of thieving.

HERNANDEZ: You must allow me to point out that for this first theft the responsibility rests with the Don Luis de Velasco whom you have seen fit to commend. Had he not destroyed the beginning Spanish colony upon the banks of the Rappahannock there would not ever have been any English settlement in Virginia, nor would Jamestown Island be burdened with a collection of serio-comic sculpture.

CABELL: He acted as befitted a patriot. I have never declared that the results of patriotism are a blessing to the world at large, nor indeed to anybody. My plea was merely that to this well-nigh forgotten Indian the indebtedness of Virginia remains greater than is its obligation to Pocahontas.

HERNANDEZ: But of a certainty you cannot put faith in the absurd hocus-pocus of Pocahontas!

CABELL: As I have granted, even in this manuscript here at my elbow, it is difficult to understand how, after having been rescued by Pocahontas in the January of 1608, John Smith could have forgotten the occurrence before the following May, when he wrote out the first account of his capture by the Indians; yet, about fifteen years afterward, he atoned handsomely for his negligence, by recollecting as many as three versions of this rescue. His apparent attack of amnesia has been accounted for upon several grounds.

HERNANDEZ: It is most easily explained by the fact

that, when John Smith returned to England in 1609, his personal friend, Richard Hakluyt, had just published a book entitled, *Virginia richly valued by the description of the maine land of Florida her next neighbor; out of four yeeres continuall travell and discoverie, for above one thousand miles east and west, of Don Ferdinando de Soto, and sixe hundred able men in his companie. Wherein are truly observed the riches and fertilitie of those parts abounding with things necessarie, pleasant, and profitable for the life of man; with the natures and dispositions of the inhabitants. Written by a Portugall gentleman of Elvas, emploied in all the action, and translated out of the Portuguese by Richard Hakluyt. At London, printed by Felix Kingston for Matthew Lownes, 1609.*

CABELL: I am not familiar with this special translation of the Gentleman of Elvas; yet the title is edifying; and I admire the powers of a memory which can recall it offhand.

HERNANDEZ: Now, in this book, which after his return to England John Smith most certainly read, one finds the story of Juan Ortiz, who in 1529 enlisted in an expedition sent into Florida by the wife of Panfilo de Narváez, in search of her missing husband. Young Ortiz was captured by the Hirrigua Indians, near Clear Water Beach; and he was then carried to the village of the chief called Ucita. There the Indians prepared to kill the white man, just as the Algonquin Indians are reported to have made ready to kill John Smith; and there, at what seemed to be the last moment of his life, Juan Ortiz was rescued by Ucita's daughter, Ulaleh, in the same manner which was attributed to Pocahontas about a century later.

CABELL: Yes; but nevertheless—

HERNANDEZ: Ortiz had many other adventures, all in the best romantic vein, during the nine years he passed among the Hirriguans: and we can imagine the chagrin with which John Smith, in reading his friend's spirited translation, observed with what ease the fine episode of this rescue by an Indian princess could have been adjusted to some one or other of the many daughters of Powhatan; but, alas, Smith's own book had been printed a few months earlier; and he was thus compelled to wait, for fifteen years, until the death of Pocahontas in England, as a figure of some casual notoriety, had afforded to him a chance to reprint selected portions of the story of Juan Ortiz as being his own story. He did not pretend to any intimacy with Pocahontas until after she had become celebrated and was safely dead.

CABELL: You are truly insatiable; for after declaring that in place of the revered name of Virginia Dare one ought to substitute the name of Martin de

Arguëlles, you attempt to convert likewise our prized Pocahontas into a Floridian. And yet what does it matter?

HERNANDEZ: Were there nothing else, this Pocahontas, even by Captain John Smith's first account—

CABELL: It so happens, I repeat, that in considering the remarkable Commonwealth of Virginia, I have not failed to appraise the *True Relation* with that painstaking completeness which befits an ethnological study. Yet my remarks are brief; and should you care to look over this manuscript here, it will confute, I believe, the still further fault-finding which you now plan.

HERNANDEZ: I fear that, what with so many interlineations and your so diminutive handwriting—

CABELL: Very truly I ought not to expect anybody except myself to decipher the hodgepodge of my manuscripts. Yet you shall not escape, through the avenue of my cramped penmanship, from being demolished. I will read aloud to you my comments upon the *True Relation*.

HERNANDEZ: I am suitably grateful.

2

CABELL: With no less of zeal than is devoted to ignoring the first Virginian, Don Luis de Velasco, do all we Virginians to whom middle-age has become a reminiscence strive to keep hugger-mugger the first book Virginia produced. We reason—through an excess of that same state-loyalty which makes us always complacent and now and then pig-headed— that inasmuch as this volume annihilates the fine tale of Pocahontas, oblivion is its right doom. And yet, to the judgment of the considerate, Captain John Smith's *True Relation* does not in any way affect the ranking of Pocahontas in the official history of Virginia; her legend, the more thanks to Virginia's unfailing good taste in mythology, has been made immortal; and so not any special hurt can arise, nowadays, from considering Virginia's first addition to literature.

One has called it, for the sake of brevity, the *True Relation*. Its birth as a book was accidental, so far as went Smith's part in it. What happened was that, in the May of 1608, Smith wrote, to an unidentified acquaintance in England, a letter as to his experiences in Virginia during the preceding twelve-month. This letter was conveyed oversea, by Captain Francis Nelson, on the *Phœnix*, in June, while Smith remained in Virginia. Of Smith's letter (which ran to the not uncustomary Jacobean length of several thousand words) a number of manuscript copies appear to have been made; and these copies were distributed among persons who shared in common, as to the infant colony, an investor's perturbed interest.

It so followed that an unbackward and thrifty economist (of whom the initials alone survive to-day), "happening upon this Relation by chance . . . thought good to publish it," during the August of 1608, after having embellished his piracy with a preface. This preface, which is signed "I. H.," admits candidly that the embezzled letter was printed "in the author's absence" and without any thought of obtaining Captain Smith's consent to its publication.

Thus casually got into type the first book to be written in Virginia; and in the orotund fashion of the age, this book was described, upon its title page, as being, *A True Relation of such occurrences and accidents of noate as hath hap'ned in Virginia since the first planting of that Collony which is now resident in the South part thereof, till the last returne from thence. Written by Captaine Smith, Coronell of the said Collony, to a worshipfull friend of his in England. London: Printed for Iohn Tappe, and are to bee solde at the Greyhounde, in Paules-Church-yard, by W. W. 1608.*

In this letter Smith records, for the first time, the now familiar story of how, in the December of 1607, John Smith was captured by a party of Indians and carried before Powhatan; and records also that "with such a grave and Majesticall countenance as drave me into admiration to see such state in a naked Salvage, hee kindly welcomed me with good wordes and great Platters of sundrie Victuals, assuring mee [of] his friendship and my libertie within foure dayes."

Whereafter, it develops, Captain Smith's enforced but uniformly agreeable visit during the first week of 1608, to King Powhatan, "in his house at Werowocomoco," was devoted for the most part to prolonged conferences between the two of them,—during which interviews Powhatan described the polity and customs and geography of his country, and questioned his hairy outland guest in regard to the tribal habits of Europe. "And thus having, with all the kindness he could devise, sought to content me"—so does Smith round off the primal story of Virginian hospitality,—"hee sent me home [that is, back to the fort at Jamestown] with 4 men—one that usually carried my Gowne and Knapsacke after me, two other[s] loded with bread, and one to accompanie me."

Such is Smith's first, confidential account of his Indian captivity and of its genial aspects. During this four days' stay at Werowocomoco he appears neither to have seen nor heard of Pocahontas. Farther on in the *True Relation*, however, he records that, in the

May of 1608—which was the same month wherein
Smith completed the letter to his "worshipfull
friend,"—"Powhatan, understanding we detained
certain Salvages, sent his Daughter, a childe of tenne
yeares old, which [daughter] not only for feature,
countenance & proportion much exceedeth any of
the rest of his people, but for wit and spirit [appears]
the only Nonpareil of his Country. This [child] he
sent by his most trustie messenger, called Rawhunt
. . . [who] with a long circumstance told mee how
well Powhatan loved and respected mee, and in
[order] that I should not doubt any way of his kindness, he had sent his child, which he most esteemed,
to see me—[and] a Deere and bread besides, for a
present. . . . His little Daughter hee had taught
this lesson also: [she] not taking notice at all of the
Indeans that had been prisoners three daies, till that
morning that she saw their fathers and friends
come, quietly and in good tearmes, to entreate their
libertie."

Smith adds that the seven captive Indians "we
. . . gave to Pocahuntas, the King's Daughter, in
regard to her father's kindness in sending her. . . .
Pocahuntas also we requited, with such trifles as
contented her, to tel that we had used the Paspa-
heyans very kindly in so releasing them."

And not anywhere else in the *True Relation* does
King Powhatan's "little Daughter," who in the May

of 1608 was "a childe of tenne yeares old," figure at all.

Here are the sole mentions of Pocahontas, as Smith put upon paper his first account of his first dealings with Pocahontas—in a private letter, as one needs to remember, wherein, if anywhere, one might suspect him of truth-telling, because there was not anything to be gained by misrepresenting what happened at Werowocomoco. And the wording of the passages which have been quoted, repays, I submit, a consideration which hitherto it has been denied, continuously.

The wording, to my judgment, proclaims, in itself, that Captain John Smith had not ever seen or heard of Pocahontas prior to the May of 1608, when the child visited Jamestown. The wording, beyond any possible doubt, shows that she here enters Smith's narrative for the first time; that in his letter she nowhere had been spoken of in any earlier passage which "I. H." omitted; and that at this point Smith is thus led, quite naturally, to explain who Pocahontas was, as well as more or less to describe her endearing small personality. The wording—if aught so obvious needs saying—forbids any least possibility that this "childe of tenne yeares old" could have been during the preceding January "twelve or thirteen yeares of age" (as she becomes in Smith's later romance vending, which requires to have her nubile), or that she had then saved from Powhatan's malignity, "at a hazard of her own life," the life of John Smith.

Pocahontas is introduced, instead, as a sprightly infant whom Smith now encounters, for the first time, at Jamestown, and whom he admires affably. Nor of course can that benign Powhatan, who "with all the kindness he could devise, sought to content me," be very readily reconciled with the improved Powhatan of Smith's heightened and matured fancies concerning a fairy-tale tyrant who was "more like a devill than a man."

The *True Relation,* in short, compels any tolerably intelligent reader to decide whether John Smith lied, quite gratuitously, about Powhatan and Pocahontas in a private letter, when he had nothing to gain by it? or whether Smith lied later, through rather more intelligible motives, during the touching up of a book of travels which he was trying to make salable? There can be, in the present low state of human nature, but one sane answer.

Nor should this answer be modified, I protest, by the fact that in the preface to the *True Relation* "I. H." remarks that "somewhat more was by him [John Smith] written, which being, I thought, fit to be private, I would not attempt to make publicke."

This, says the ever loyal Virginian—and how very often has he repeated his glib *non sequitur*, with an heroic stubbornness!—must of necessity refer to the rescue by Pocahontas; but he does not trouble to explain for what reason "I. H.," in pirating the book for his own private profit, should have chosen to leave out the most striking parts of it; nor above all, does the Virginian pause to reflect that, in any such improbable case, the entire narrative of the *True Relation* must have been rewritten and recolored before it was published.

The impossibility that this episode was left out is shown, in brief, by the impossibility of putting it back in. Nobody, I submit, could do that without contradicting the rest of the story as we here have it. To interject into Smith's high panegyric of a courteous and large-hearted monarch, who displayed unfailingly, throughout four days, "all the kindness he could devise," an account of how the same monarch, upon this or the other of these days, gave orders that the brains of his guest should be dashed out with a bludgeon would border—one somehow feels—upon the discrepant. Nor is it conceivable that Smith could have written anything at all like his portrayal of Pocahontas as it stands today in the *True Relation* if ever, even once, he had mentioned this "childe of tenne yeares old" anywhere earlier in the complete text of his letter.

And in passing, one finds it noteworthy that a wholly credible and unprejudiced witness, who did not suspect Pocahontas of intending to become a heroine of romance, even somewhat lessens those first fatal figures which Smith gave as to the child's age. William Strachey, Secretary of the Colony, records that in the May of 1610, when he arrived at Jamestown, Pocahontas had not yet assumed the leathern loincloth which would have proclaimed her twelfth birthday; and he tells likewise how this "well featured but wanton young girle" then embarrassed the British, by exhibiting to everybody her private parts naked, when Pocahontas was turning handsprings about the fort at Jamestown, with a sportiveness not entirely suited to the great-grandmother of so many leading Virginians.

Even so, it is perhaps my duty to add that this alleged public display of the pudenda of Pocahontas has been afforded a figleaf through the assertion that Powhatan had, "no doubt," two daughters called Pocahontas. I am deterred only by the reflection that neither Powhatan nor anyone of his contemporaries appears ever to have noted this fact; as well as by the yet further reflection that this figleaf was applied, with a chaste deference, by the same native Virginian historian who discovered intrepidly, without needing any mere evidence to abet him, that, "no doubt," every one of the jailbirds transported into the Colony of Virginia, during the period of its establishment, had been convicted unjustly. Into the better-thought-of accounts of our commonwealth one does not permit the base intrusions of common-sense.

So then does the *True Relation* demolish faith in the romantic story of Pocahontas as an actual occurrence. It shows that at Werowocomoco this infant did not rescue Captain John Smith from being murdered at her father's orders, or from any other perils. It attests that, later on, John Smith, as a capable and painstaking historian, either invented or else borrowed the entire affair.

—No one of which drab facts, I repeat, can in any way affect the unshakable position of Pocahontas in the official history of Virginia. She at all hazards remains one of its brighter ornaments; she is of a piece with the rest of it, by and large; and through the peculiar favor of Heaven—which has granted to every loyal Virginian "of the old school" an ability to believe neither more nor less by one hair's breadth than that which he elects to believe—her picturesque legend has been made immortal.

And for one, I commend this outcome, without any reservation of any nature, because of my liking for the official history of Virginia as a work of art, "in the more freely interpretative form of fiction."

3

HERNANDEZ: Your paper, to the best of my knowledge as a professor of history, is both accurate and injudicious.

CABELL: I thank you. I had meant simply to convey that, in private, the not illiterate Virginian will grant Smith's improvising as to Pocahontas—as well as to a great number of other affairs. And only when he is writing history, or in the delivery of a commemorative address, does a Virginian attempt to justify the quaint juggling of time and geography, and of nomenclature, through which the daughter of Ananias Dare is ranked as a daughter of "the Colony of Virginia."

HERNANDEZ: One might as well expect a Virginian to justify his twin boasts that, just as in this continent Virginia was the first English colony, so during the American Revolution was Virginia the main agent in causing all our Atlantic seaboard to cease being an English colony. If either one of these entities is to be counted praiseworthy, then the other would seem to be reprehensible.

CABELL: My dear friend, but you who derive from Spain, by way of Minorca, cannot well understand how volatile is the moral nature of our more variable English stock. In Virginia we, who share in this national trait, can make for it a correct allowance.

We know in Virginia that the English remained paragons of all manly virtues from the accession of King Arthur until about 1765,—when overnight, as it were, those cousins whom we had left behind in England became churlish taskmasters, and attempted to impose upon us taxation without representation, very nearly two centuries before we were prepared to accept it.

HERNANDEZ: Yes; but, as I was saying—

CABELL: Their conduct yet again, prior to and during the War of 1812, when they pressganged our citizens, and burned the White House, and demolished the Capitol of the United States, was not exemplary. When, as we Virginians phrased it, they betrayed the Confederacy—under the darkling influence of a German Prince Consort—then we for some while compared them with Iscariot to the marked advantage of Judas. But in 1914, or thereabouts, when on a sudden our reformed kinsmen became the champions of all oppressed countries which were not a remunerative part of the British Empire, they regained their temporarily mislaid excellence.

HERNANDEZ: Yes; but if you will permit me to observe—

CABELL: They relapsed into unpopularity during the 1920's, it is true, when they decided to repay their war debts in a coinage of epithets and jeers.

In Virginia we did not relish this mimicking of our own financial exploits after the War Between the States. It appeared almost rude. Yet this example of extreme thrift is now an affair of the past. We have pardoned everything because of that generosity with which, after Dunkerque, the English agreed to share with us all our belongings.

HERNANDEZ: Yes; but your phrasing of the matter—

CABELL: So I remark only that everywhere in Virginia we rejoice today that we are Anglo-Saxon, even if we are not. "We are proud"—or so, at least, I have read in the high periods of a former Governor of Virginia—"to be joint heirs in every Anglo-Saxon's priceless heritage of splendid deeds, which illumine forever the pathway of human progress and endeavor. We are proud of the rock from which we are hewn. We are proud to speak the language of Shakespeare and Milton"—as well as, of course, of Hengist and Beowulf. Such is the faith of every loyal Virginian in regard to our English forebears; and when rightly appraised, it is alike simple and natural.

HERNANDEZ: Yes; but to my finding, it is more than simple; for it is feeble-minded.

4

CABELL: And I can but repeat, What does it matter? It is the fault of you historians—in Florida as well as in all other states except only one state—that you concern yourselves to a suicidal extent (I mean, from art's standpoint) with affairs of fact. How very differently do we shape our history in Virginia, where we accept such facts as we find desirable and dismiss those which are not to our purpose! We have thus enriched the field of American folklore with that stirring epic which is the history of Virginia; nor will any virtuoso of art deny that in its splendor of fancy, in its wealth of heart-warming patriotism, and in its high flights of imagination, it very far excels the history of any other commonwealth.

Yet art has its own rules; and art declines to be hampered by the untoward accident that not until 1609 was a white child born in the present State of Virginia. This Virginia Laydon was the daughter of a mere carpenter, to begin with, through the indulgence of a house maid; nor does anything in particular seem ever to have happened to this Virginia Laydon. She is thus not to our purpose; she is not poetic material.

And so, in place of her, we have a strong need, such as transcends the calendar and prosaic state lines, to begin our great epic with the fable of Virginia Dare, who, in addition to her far more suitable social rank as the granddaughter of the governor of the colony, was likewise the first child to be born of English parents upon this continent. Along with the entire Roanoke Colony she disappeared, it is not known how or through what agency, between 1588 and 1591; and this unexplained vanishing is in accord with all the very best traditions of folklore, inasmuch as it may be taken to involve the supreme mystery of the atonement, by which the innocent are sacrificed in order to secure the tribe's welfare.

As I need hardly remind you, this sacrifice of the first-born child is a religious custom which always has been held in world-wide reverence. You will recall that this custom formerly prevailed among the Timucuan Indians of your Florida, just as among the Phœnicians and the Jews— But I desist. You should thank me.—For I might here become pedantic as to a vast number of yet other peoples who practiced this custom in every quarter of the globe; I might even venture into theology by citing mystics who in the Crucifixion have seen Jehovah confirming this custom through the sacrifice of His first and only Son as the needed price of His peoples' welfare; but I spare you any such obvious reflections.

I remark merely that the gracious if vague figure of Virginia Dare is felt, by instinct perhaps rather than by reason, to be, like Iphigenia, the first-born child that has been offered and found acceptable as a bribe to secure Heaven's kindliness toward her people now that her people have begun a vast enterprise. As the daughter of King Agamemnon bought Troy for the Greeks, so did the granddaughter of Governor John White buy Virginia for her own people through the divine favor which was purchased by her immolation. (That her people could not have been North Carolinians is proved, in passing, by the fact that nobody ever heard of any divine favor shown toward North Carolinians.) I do not say that this analogue is good logic, but merely that it is sound poetry. Virginia Dare disappeared in the arcane manner of Iphigenia; and perhaps, still like Iphigenia, she became a priestess among tribes no less strange and savage than were the Tauri. So at least runs one of our legends. No more than at Aulis the Greeks knew what had become of Iphigenia, may we of Virginia imagine what became of Virginia Dare. We know only that through her sacrifice the epic of Virginia has been begun in a correct manner such as satisfied the requirements of art.

And of Pocahontas also we have need in our epic, if but only because her story figures in all other well-thought-of mythologies. The legend of Pocahontas appears in every known land. That, as seems not improbable, Smith may have founded his special version of it upon an actual occurrence in the life of Juan Ortiz, we may very well concede without argument, inasmuch as Smith could have obtained the tale from hundreds of other sources. He might have borrowed it from the romance of Huon of Bordeaux, or from the fable of Gilbert à Becket (who, with the assistance of a Mohammedan Pocahontas somewhat surprisingly called "Susy Pye," begot St. Thomas of Canterbury), or else from "The Loving Ballad of Lord Bateman."

Everywhere in folklore does one find this story, of a young man in the power of a ruthless foreign captor, whose daughter falls in love with and releases the prisoner from the cruelty of her father— with the father appearing, variously, as a gaoler, an emperor, a fiend, a sultan, a god, a giant, or a sorcerer —and with varying sequels. In Andrew Lang's *Custom and Myth* one notes an exceedingly long list of the prototypes of Smith's story, "ranging from Finland to Japan, from Samoa to Madagascar, from Greece to India." The true point is not at all that Smith plagiarized his story, but the fact that in our Virginian mythology Pocahontas has her fit place, and that, howsoever she became enshrined there, the event was praiseworthy.

So Pocahontas remains, as one of our more characteristic Virginian authors has remarked, "a forest rose, diffusing a sweet odor of the rarest virtues, and forever fragrant in the memory of Virginia." Nor does my compatriot omit to prophesy—as to this "child of the forest, though daughter of an emperor, and scion of a savage race, yet mother of a sterling Christian stock"—that the redolence of her loyal womanhood will forever refresh the pages of history.

He points out that though English royalty claimed Pocahontas as its favorite, and a Briton took her from the wilderness to be his wife, she is nevertheless "the peculiar heritage and the lasting pride of Virginia." He admits that her mortal remains have mingled with the dust of Albion, far away from the leafy haunts of her dark forebears; but (so does my fellow-Virginian conclude) this Sylvan Maid yet lives in all our memories, throughout the entire state, even from Accomac County to Lee County, as a type of everything which can make her gentle sex most lovable.

That, in Virginia, my dear Hernandez, is considered the correct historical attitude toward the several thousand years old myth of Pocahontas. It defies, I submit, any seriously intended criticism.

5

HERNANDEZ: You have silenced me, indeed, with an impressive jumble of Virginian logic and of Virginian rhetoric. Yet I still believe the historian should record truth without titivation. It is to this theory at least that we historians have conformed in our Florida.

CABELL: And with what depressing results, you must allow me to remark, even where the raw materials of your art were unrivaled! You have chosen in Florida to romanticize your climate rather than your past. Yet the history of Florida, in mere point of fact, is more interesting than that of any other state in the Union; the history of Virginia does not compare with it in variety or color or drama, nor even, let it be whispered, in antiquity; but the history of Florida has not ever been handled with the poetic abandon which graces all our accounts of Virginia. The history of Florida has not ever been humanized.

HERNANDEZ: It at least contains a few facts.

CABELL: It cannot even boast of containing a few facts; for in all the formal histories of Florida which are known to me, one encounters thousands of facts, as to religious differences, and treaties, and sieges, and political requirements, and alligators, and massacres, and steam boats, and foreign policies, and hotels, and railways, and the citrus industry. The sole drawback is that one does not encounter any men and women—such as throng everywhere in the history of Virginia.

HERNANDEZ: Now, there you exaggerate—

72

CABELL: But, no, my dear friend: I protest to you that excepting only one volume which dealt with the St. Johns River, and as to the demerits and heresies of which I am not a competent judge, I have found in no existent account of Florida any outright suggestion that the peninsula was ever inhabited by human beings. There are merely names, and then yet more names, to which the writer who lists them has failed to attach any personality.

HERNANDEZ: Ah, but nevertheless—

CABELL: So-and-so did this or the other, we are told: that is all. It is almost as if from a long since out-of-date telephone book one were reading a selection of the subscribers' names and occupations. Or rather, it is as if, in some gray underworld, one confronted a horde of but half-seen and featureless ghosts who stray confusedly, through a twilight of syntax, about an endless flatness of diction. So does it follow that nobody can manage to toil through the reading of a history of Florida except under compulsion; and that not merely in my native state, but in many other places, very few persons suspect that Florida has any history at all. But to every literate English-speaking person the spirited romance of the founding of Virginia has been made familiar.

HERNANDEZ: I notice that your glass is empty.

6

CABELL: I thank you. —For in Virginia, I can but repeat, we shape our history with discretion, in the same instant that we decline to stint the higher needs of our patriotism by accepting anything one whit short of the most edifying and pleasing history. When outsiders babble that a great deal of this history did not ever happen, they speak beside the mark. The past is done with; but our beliefs as to the past endure. Upon all imaginable counts, it is far better that these beliefs should be agreeable and inspiring and magnanimous; and that they should so prompt us to live in a manner not unworthy of our forefathers.

That these forefathers were in reality a rather commonplace set—and far more that they were a gang of thieving opportunists—would be a creed from which none could derive any profit, but only discouragement. And no history is a matter of record; it is a matter of faith.

The great epic of Virginia's settlement may not have occurred precisely as Virginians narrate it; yet that suspicion may be raised likewise as to the *Odyssey* and the *Æneid* without prompting us to contemn any one of these three masterworks. Sceptics have doubted, for example, the story of Dido and Æneas merely because Dido could not have been

born until long after the death of Æneas; and upon
the futile ground that many of the doings of Odysseus
are impossible, sciolists have refrained from believ-
ing in every one of his exploits completely. We are
not concerned by such nonsense; we instead read
with contentment; and finding everywhere in the
work of genius so much which no human intelligence, it seems, could have invented, we deduce
unavoidably that all these things did happen.

It is well for us to revere that handful of intrepid
Englishmen who cast off the oppression and corrup-
tion of the Old World in order to secure freedom,
alike of conscience and action, and who thus founded
at Jamestown a new nation, than which, as every
one of our native historians has remarked, and so
forth and so on. Even that cultured sceptic who of
all celebrated Virginians was the least given to in-
discriminate enthusiasm has observed, as to the settlers of Jamestown, that "their free and valiant spirit
gave birth to all that is free and valiant in our history. They lived and died that a small adventure
might become a great cause of liberty, and a country without a name the foremost republic in the
world."

It were idle to reply that the London Company
for Virginia was appreciably less interested in
founding a republic—even a republic than which
and so forth and so on—than in securing dividends

for its stockholders; or that, in mere point of fact, pretty much every Englishman concerned in the Jamestown venture would have resented with muskets the notion of a republic; for reflection assures us that to believe any event whatsoever did not happen in just the way that we find it to be recorded by the piety and the scholarship of Virginia, is but the same pedantic frivolity which would declare the *Odyssey* or the *Æneid* to be implausible.

To investigate the noble epic of Virginia's settlement in the bleak light of common-sense, or of mere probability, is, not only for the Virginian, but for every correct-thinking American, to repeat the sin of Ham. It is not wise for us to uncover the nakedness of our forefathers. We have no need to know the exact physical truth about them, but we do have an exceedingly strong need of those high ideals which, even if they did not pursue or ever hear about any such ideals, they have bequeathed to us through our Virginian version of Virginia's history. To impugn this version is to rob ourselves of our own legacy and, like less long-headed Esaus, to lose our birthright without getting so much as a mess of pottage in exchange. It is, in brief, a sacrilege combined with unthrift, and a fatuity such as no person can avoid with a caution too painstaking. But I notice that the bottle is empty.

Part Three ❧

COLONEL ESMOND OF VIRGINIA

Their deeds live after them enshrined in imperishable treasure-houses of minstrelsy, song and story; and so here is to the men and women who have remembered the dreams that inspired Virginia's planting; who have held in heart the achievements of her great men; who have lifted glad eyes to the place of her tree-clad mountains, her joyous fields and her sunny, wave-kissed shores; and who, by the strength and witchery of record and rhyme, of history, romance and poem, have builded a myriad-windowed temple of letters, exquisite, luminous, enduring, for all the world to see.

ANNE PENDLETON

1

ALTHOUGH Virginia may have produced a fair number of writers as to whom the fond pride of Virginia, if not any actual purchase of their books, might appear justifiable, you, Sir, were the first among them in merit. Of them all, you remain the most widely gifted, the most urbane, and the most delectable. 'Tis therefore an unaccountable fact that you should stay uncommemorated in every formal list of Virginia's greater glories.

Unaccountable, I repeat, because no few Virginians are sufficiently literate to know that when in 1718 you settled at Castlewood in Westmoreland County, you became, for the remaining thirty years of your traditional threescore and ten, a Virginian; and that 'twas in the Northern Neck of Virginia, be tween the years 1718 and 1736, you completed your Memoirs—although but so far as to the date of your immigration—in a fine volume now everywhere delighted in by the judicious.

Through some mischance, of a nature which hath not ever been explained, these Memoirs languished in manuscript until 1852, when Mr. W. M. Thackeray (who was himself a writer of pretty fair English, for a native of Calcutta) then edited your life's history, with a reprovable amount of inattention. Nevertheless did your Memoirs, howsoever liberally bespotted by editorial blottings, then demonstrate that a Virginian, when he once puts his mind to it, can write English prose such as no Englander, whether British or New, hath ever excelled. They revealed you as the supreme artist in Virginian letters.

Of your other writings but little is known. Your occasional verses, "To Gloriana," as these appeared in the *Observator*, in 1705, stay inedited. 'Tis believed that no example of your one dramatic piece, *The Faithful Fool*, outlasted the author's own copy, which perished, it is said, when Castlewood, in common with Wakefield, was burned down (each mansion even to its cellarage) during the Christmas week of 1780. We know merely that this comedic essay was found praiseworthy by critics no less eminent than Mr. John Dennis and Captain Richard Steele.

2

YET time hath spared to us your Memoirs; and in reading them, we of necessity must grieve that you did not stretch so far toward posterity your friendship as to include the affairs of your middle life and old age in Virginia—of which, to your fellow-enthusiasts for what's bygone, an authentic record would be of deep interest, in a commonwealth so very generally devoted to all nature of antiquities that to manufacture them hath become, of late years, its chief enterprise, some scoffers sneer.

I dismiss, Sir, these vipers to their proper pit. I remark merely that 'tis strange to observe how infrequent, even in the main repository of our state's archives, in Richmond, are the surviving mentions of Henry Esmond's name. For was it not to your judgment, first of all ("as being most ripe in this World's Affairs of any Gentleman now in Virginia"), that Colonel William Byrd submitted the earliest known mention of his plan to establish this same Richmond, in a reply to your so nicely critical commendation of the rough draft for his *History of the Dividing Line?*

"It may seem like a Joke when I tell you that I have not Time to finish that work," wrote Colonel Byrd, with a modest author's not immitigable nonchalance as to the genius displayed by his labors. "But 'tis very [certain] I have not, for I am always engaged on some project for improving our Infant Colony. The present scheme is to found a city at the Falls of James River, and plant a colony of Switzers on my Land upon Roanoke." Nothing came of the latter project; or, rather, the Switzers went to South Carolina, where they fared unprosperingly; but from the first scheme (of which we may assume you approved) sprang Richmond.

3

ALTHOUGH of the historic circumstance that you pretty constantly frequented young Richmond my lean scholarship hath unearthed no positive record, yet I find the outcome to be incredible that persons who so often visited Westover as did Colonel Esmond and his daughter, Madam Esmond Warrington, should not have inspected the new town near by, again and yet again. You did not meet Colonel Byrd, it is true, until his return from England in 1726, nor did the acquaintance thrive after Mrs. Warrington's lamentable quarrel with Mrs. Thomas Chamberlayne, of King William County, his second daughter.

The scandal which Mrs. Warrington then spread abroad is a story too sad and startling to be repeated in this place; I dare report merely that it accredited Mrs. Chamberlayne with a then unmodish tolerance of racial equality, even after bed time. Nobody, however (as little Madam Esmond Warrington admitted, continuously and with a malign benevolence, to all the upper circles of Virginia), needed to wonder over the misconduct of a London goldsmith's granddaughter. —For such tradespeople as were the Byrds of Westover had their own queer tastes when it came to Negroes; and about any such disgusting matters the gentry preferred to remain silent, as Mrs. Warrington repeated over and yet over again. She in this way prevented any further exchange of amenities between the Byrds and the Esmonds.

Prior to this regrettable outcome, you had been much at Westover. Indeed, avows tradition, 'twas in the East Parlour of Westover that (as Mrs. Warrington records) a wine-emboldened gentleman from York County, said to have been one of the Ballards, was guilty of the unparalleled offence of treating Colonel Esmond with levity,—"and I am bound to own," she adds, "that my papa never forgave him."

One imagines also that you were very often to be seen, upon parade, as it were, in the Palace at Williamsburg, as a prized ornament of the current Governor's levée. With Lieutenant-Governor Spotswood alone you could not be hoped to get on amenably, because of his loud devotion to the great Duke of Marlborough, whom you had served under and abhorred. So you did not return to Germanna after the September evening in 1736, when "Colo. Spotswood received us very courteously. And lest we should have forgot the memorable Battles of the Duke of Marlborough, he fought them all over again to us for the nine and fortieth time."

To this caustic précis you have added nothing: one comprehends, nevertheless, that of Alexander Spotswood, as the misguided admirer of a personage who had once snubbed Henry Esmond in public, your verbal portrait, had you ever attempted it, would have been etched with strong acids implacably. Truly was it said of you—by a great, bright splendid minx—that although you never fell into a passion, yet you never forgave.

4

'Tis with an arrogant greed, perhaps, we lament that, in addition to the richness and the ever-prodigal opulence of your Memoirs, you did not grant to Virginia likewise the large bounty of depicting your life in Virginia. Still, Sir, one cannot but regard those unrecorded thirty years with some unavoidable curiosity. One would very much like to know, for example, how your marriage "to the truest and tenderest and purest wife ever man was blessed with" did turn out, in point of fact, as an everyday arrangement.

We honor the exalted terminal rhapsodies of your Memoirs, which are so thoroughly in the most happy vein of Southern chivalry as to reflect no whit less of credit upon your heart than on your rhetoric; but after all, we do remember that your Rachel was of an incurably jealous disposition and a good eight years older than you were. That special combination would not seem to make over-strongly for connubial bliss. We quite honestly hope, in fine, that always, after your marriage at Bruxelles, Colonel and Mrs. Henry Esmond "billed and cooed like a pair of old pigeons on a perch." But we rather doubt it.

At all events, when in England she visited her elder daughter, then Mrs. Thomas Tusher, I am indissuadably certain you were not permitted to make one of the party. Instead, you stayed quietly in your London lodgings, smoking a great deal that day. Your returning wife reported to you that dear poor Beatrix had lost all her good looks and become stout disgustingly. You shrugged. You assumed a discreet sympathizing. You declared at once, patting lightly the back of Mrs. Esmond's lean spotted hand, that no other woman could hope to defy time's malice with the success of your Rachel.

But tacitly you remembered, as you could not but forever remember, your twenty-fourth birthday— that magical twenty-ninth of December which you spent at Walcote, when Ensign Esmond, then of Quin's regiment of Fusileers, who had last seen Beatrix as a child, found her to be a woman "arrived at a dazzling perfection of beauty," and lost his brave heart to her for all time.

She came down the hall stairway to meet you, your Memoirs record. She carried a lighted taper. She wore scarlet stockings with silver clocks to them. And then the company went in to supper, just the four Esmonds, to celebrate Ensign Harry's happy return from the battle of Vigo Bay. That was all. Nothing else whatever happened at Walcote during that far-off wintry evening. Yet the diversities and the bland, amplified, tip-tilted cadences of your prose have made of these simple events an unearthly adventuring, a strange bright sortie which enters into faëry land, triumphantly.

How in the world did you ever do it? we lesser Virginian writers cannot but humbly wonder today. The implements of your magic are nowhere discernible; and yet the magic is there, in the form of a most strong magic, of a resistless love-philtre, which has rendered all literate persons forever enamoured of young Beatrix Esmond.

5

HERE I avert from this special theme, if but because I have no desire, Sir, to become in the rhapsodic your outrivaled competitor. I address myself to more practical ends. I state simply, as the true purpose of this open letter, that to the considerate who believe your Memoirs to be the best narrative ever produced in

Virginia, it would seem imperative, in this not un-profitable era of Virginian restorations, for a cor-rected and augmented version of your masterwork to be issued, with the over-many editorial blunders of Mr. Thackeray either removed or emended.

His slips shriek to Heaven. They begin indeed with the very preface, in which, upon 3 November 1778, Mrs. Warrington is familiar with the outcome of the American Revolution some three years later and the establishment of our Republic in 1789; yet appears ignorant of her half-sister's second mar-riage, with the Baron de Bernstein, at least thirty years prior to the date when Rachel Esmond War-rington wrote her preface—under the odd delusion, in passing, that her own late husband was "but the younger son of a Suffolk Baronet," whereas the War-rington family, 'tis certain, graced the County of Norfolk. Moreover, Madam Esmond Warrington had maintained some correspondence with Madame de Bernstein; and according to her own memoranda, had sent to "Baroness Bernstein," in the October of 1756, four jars of preserved peaches and six hams, "per the *Royal William* of Liverpool."

These facts are made plain by the Memoirs of your elder grandson, Sir George Esmond Warring-ton, as in 1857 they likewise were edited, by the graceful lax hand of Mr. Thackeray, under the title of *The Virginians*—a volume, by the bye, in which a great deal of uncalled for anguish arises out of the circumstance that it doth not occur to Mr. Thackeray how very easily your descendants, when threatened with an eviction from Castlewood-in-Virginia, could have obtained from the county records of our Westmoreland, which date from 1653, a duly certified copy of the misplaced deed by which your estates in the Northern Neck had been conveyed to you by your stepson.

One might marshal here a cohort of yet further self-contradictions and unlikelihoods; but it suffices to report that everywhere this Mr. Thackeray, when his editorship faces a matter of chronology or of accurateness, hath heaped upon the inconsistent the impossible. So a restoration of your true eighteen-century text, I stay certain, would be a pleasant and praiseworthy task for some one of our patriotic Virginian organizations.

In that happy event, your Memoirs might be dealt with upon the same generous principles which have governed most of our restorations in Virginia. I mean that, just as at Williamsburg, for an instance, in restoring the famous Wren Building (*open daily 9—5, small fee to guide*), was added to it a desirable and complete south wing which the original edifice did not ever possess—except only, perhaps, in Sir Christopher Wren's discarded plans, which were not followed in erecting the so-called Wren Building in its first form, or in the revamped, restored version either—so then to your restored Memoirs could be added all that which you, at least imaginably, may have sketched out in your own discarded plans.

Your personal record of the last thirty years or so of Henry Esmond's life in Virginia might thus be restored, through skilled daily labor furnished by the Authors' League of America, into an existence which fact never gave to this desirable complete record; and still another fine relic of Virginia's prime, not at all impaired by time's passing, could be manufactured in this manner within the next month or two.

6

I AM not unaware, dear Sir, that graceless souls as yet encumber this earth who deny that, in the edifice which an admired gentlewoman hath described as being our commonwealth's most "exquisite and luminous and enduring and myriad-windowed temple of letters," your Memoirs are the corner-stone. 'Tis merely that, as befits a Virginian, I do not ever heed any carping twaddle of this nature, such as jealousy and deficient imaginations have but too often upraised against the more highly cherished antiquities of Virginia.

There is in Surry County, for example, the handsome "Rolfe Property House" (*open 9—5 daily: adm. 25c*), which in 1935 our Association for the Preservation of Virginia Antiquities restored lavishly, and put upon exhibition as having been the aforetime home of the sole son of our incomparable Pocahontas, Mr. Thomas Rolfe. Though such iniquity may be difficult of belief, yet by-and-by did wicked persons, a coterie of mere fiends in the drab form of antiquaries, make public their undesired proofs—which, for that matter, are still suffered to remain impiously upon open record at Surry Court House—that this revered residence was, instead, builded and occupied by one Mr. Thomas Warren, a burgess for Surry County; and that the "Rolfe Property House" was never at any season owned by Thomas Rolfe, nor by any other member of the Rolfe family.

Well, and to what results, after all, doth such babbling attain? We of Virginia whom fate hath blessed with correct principles have but to agree—without any more display of anger than befits the well-bred —that persons who betray to public knowledge any such inconvenient facts are not loyal Virginians. We can then dismiss all such outcasts unheeded. We do: and the Rolfe stage-property house continues to assess, and to delight, the amateur of Virginia's history "in the more freely interpretative form of fiction."

7

GRANTING that Mr. Thackeray did restore through his own private enterprise your Memoirs, in 1852, they would yet antedate becomingly the reputed stage of your later life, our restored Williamsburg, as that bric-a-brac but instructive subsidiary of the Standard Oil Company of New Jersey hath been renovated into antiquity during recent times. (*Combination tickets, at $1.50 each, can now be obtained, at the Craft House, providing admission to all exhibition buildings of Colonial Williamsburg, Inc.; 75c for children.*)

Nay, Sir, but let us dare to outface the problem in its most ebon aspect. For the noble sake of tumbling dustward the abominable, let us fancy your Memoirs to be a mere Wardour Street confection throughout, even such as (snarl the enviers of Virginia) is Williamsburg. Let us imagine, howsoever wildly, that in 1852 Mr. Thackeray invented your Memoirs, every word of them, from "The actors in the old tragedies" down to "the tenderest heart in the world."

Wherein, even then (I demand of your benign and all-accomplished shade as well as of the welkin) can their validity differ from the validity of your Castlewood's twin manor in Westmoreland, our restored Wakefield, which of late years hath de-

servedly become in all Virginia's bright treasury of
paste jewels the supreme gem? ——For indeed, Sir, inasmuch as your Memoirs, if they were not completed
until 1852, would still be a fair eighty years more
ancient than is the historic and venerable mansion
house at Wakefield, which piety begot upon imagination in 1932, to asperse your writings' antiquity
would seem to belittle also the antiquity of your
esteemed neighbor's, young George Washington's,
current first home.

To vent blasphemy as to this national shrine, the
world-famous Birthplace of Washington (*open 8 to
6; adm. 10c*), could not but be regarded, by the sage
Virginian, as a criminal folly and mere moon-struck
sedition. 'Tis beyond reason to pick flaws in a relic
so impressive and remunerative, upon the shallow
ground that our first President's birthplace was not
builded until two centuries after his birth; for his
genius triumphed over all difficulties.

So do I infer, from the implausibility of any such
lewd babblings about Wakefield, or about Colonial
Williamsburg, Inc., or about the "Rolfe Property
House," that your Memoirs, whatsoever their source,
may be ranked as a sound example of Virginiana,
not to be caviled at. And it follows—as through this
same open letter, I would deferently suggest to the
civic pride of our commonwealth at large—that Virginia should add forthwith to its superb long list of

priorities the distinction of having brought forth also —in *The History of Henry Esmond, Esq., Written by Himself*—the first, if not indeed the sole, first-class narrative ever produced in America.

Our backwardness in this grave matter (as I made bold to observe at the start of my own counterfeit antique) is an unaccountable omission which sins equally against your merits and our customary procedure. So I doubt not it may shortly be remedied; and I look forward toward a complete restoration of your Memoirs into a rather more gaudy compliance with our quaint great state's not ever dying love for all forms of freedom—a very special virtue which through our latter-day invention of Virginia's antiquities we have displayed, I submit, at its noble utmost.

Part Four ৡ

CONCERNS HEIRS AND ASSIGNS

It is the hall mark of every mortal champion that he should leave his wonted home, and the faces which are known, to go in search of what is remote and strange to him. He meets with improbable happenings. Then the tall lad returns home. He has done with the rough and tumble of foreign travel. Amid the acclaim of his neighbors he settles down to domestic life, and he lives (we are told in the folklore of primitive nations) happily ever afterward.

THESE RESTLESS HEADS

1

Wʜᴇɴ in speaking of our Virginian version of Virginia's history, and of our free-handed improvement upon the relics of Virginia's past, I observed that an appreciable deal of the resultant romance is not a matter of record, but entirely a matter of faith, I did not mean to imply that in this special respect we Virginians are unique. The case is far otherwise. In every known country which is sufficiently civilized to depend upon explosives as an expression of its ideals, the traditions which humankind in general agree to accept as history have contrived alike to defy and to embellish a number of certified facts; so that almost everywhere history is to be seen thumbing her nose at historians.

It is an unladylike habit as to which I incline to speak with some personal concern; and which here guides me into recording my own failure as an historian, impurely and simply, on account of my not handling the past after the improving manner of Virginia.

I begin this act of humiliation by admitting that in the trilogy which consists of *Hamlet Had an Uncle, The King Was in His Counting House,* and *The First Gentleman of America,* each tale has been plagiarized from recorded events. Every one of these three stories did actually happen in very much the same way that I have narrated it, or else a distressingly huge number of revered if not often read historians have all tarradiddled. Such is my first, main, and essential point.

So far as goes my collective title, I submit, the fact ought to be apparent, to any student who approaches history with a proper painstaking, that in each unit of this trilogy the story, howsoever variously handled—as a saga, and as a melodrama, and as folklore—stays at bottom the same; and that it thus illustrates history's not uncelebrated habit of repeating itself.

This thrice used scenario, as contrived by Jehovah, and by me borrowed, has been summarized to the best of my ability in the preface to the first written of these historical studies, *The King Was in His Counting House*. The protagonist of each book, after his allotted jaunt, with youth to incite him, into outlandish regions, accepts more or less willingly his allotted place in the social organism of his own people and country. That, and that merely, is my plot.

2

I REMARK here that this deferred compromise (upon which Christ also has founded a parable) appears to have been the normal story of every man ever since Cain, toward middle life, established the city of Enoch and settled down to its governance. So you may call this omnipresent story, just as you elect, either a truism or an eternal verity. It, in any case, is the story of Wiglerus, and of Cesario dei Vetori, and of Don Luis de Velasco, in my three historical studies. The would-be nonconformist is compelled, by-and-by, to accept in this world his decreed heritage, whether as an heir or an assign; and he accepts likewise the requirements, the enforced requirements, of his heritage.

This, I repeat, is the story of every human being who is not fated to die in youth or in prison. There is none who survives to reach middle-age but has learned, in one way or another, to accept in this world his inheritance. Time teaches us, indeed, that almost all human living is an exercise of acceptance rather than of action; and a career (as H. G. Wells, I believe, once phrased this matter) far less of doing things than of having things done to you. We are not born of our own volition, nor as the rule are our preferences consulted about dying; and between these two imposed necessities there is not much which a considerate person can believe to be performed of his own will unalloyed.

In all forms of civilization you at every moment face the same choice; you can conform to the notions advocated by your neighbors or else you will be destroyed by these notions. It sounds ignoble; and yet, in flesh-and-blood practice, it works out surprisingly well, because as the Grand Inquisitor declares to Christ, in Dostoevsky's harsh fine fable, "Man is tormented by no greater anxiety than to find quickly someone to whom he can hand over that gift of freedom with which the ill-fated creature is born."

3

IN OUR former republic, as one notes admiringly, this axiom has been proved to perfection. For wellnigh a century and a half, Americans had put up with personal independence as they best might; and the savage customs of the United States were tolerated but shruggingly by civilized peoples. In fact, as I recall the barbaric, strange free Commonwealth of Virginia in which I was reared, it seems that under this naïve régime you were allowed to do anything by which your immediate neighbors were not annoyed beyond reasonable endurance; and you lived for months, or for years even, without direct contact with any law, whether federal or state or civic.

Then, with the first of our successful wars to end all wars, we attained the experience of being supervised continually by law; and finding it, upon the whole, a comfort, we fell victim to the newly discovered drug. We became enamoured of questionnaires. We delighted in restrictions. We craved more and yet more legal enactments such as would not merely prevent us from doing so-and-so but would compel us to do this, that, or the other, at an appointed season; and would thus liberate us from the mental struggle of choice and rejection which freedom involves.

Not by beneficent demagogues, as some hasty persons have inferred, were we guided toward the sound equilibrium of serfdom, but through self-election we builded lovingly a strong prison in which we could all be confined; we forged our own shackles with enthusiasm; and we are still making yet more many our defences against the personal freedom of any loyal citizen, so that in the concourse of civilized nations the United States of America may be enrolled as an harmonious unit.

America, in brief, during my own time, has followed out very much the same course which in the end was pursued by each one of my three protagonists in these three historical studies; and has thus illustrated, upon a gratifyingly large scale, the truth of my thesis. One appreciates such consideration by one's own people.

4

As CONCERNS the historical base of *The King Was in His Counting House*, I confess to delinquency. When this book was published, I admitted that its main events were taken from history, but I ought to have explained also that in this narrative my plan was to remove Cosimo dei Medici, once Duke of Florence, and after 1569 the first Grand Duke of Tuscany, along with his not stainless home circle, from out of their native Italy, into the more active and vivid "Italy" of Jacobean drama.

It was a country to which, rather oddly, this especial branch of the house of Medici stayed unacclimated. No Jacobean dramatist has used this story, so far as I know, except only the fragment of it which Thomas Middleton employs in his *Women Beware Women*. In his genial if mortuary melodrama (somewhat unaccountably involved with a group of characters borrowed from a then popular novel, which in England was one of the best sellers during the autumn season of 1627) are to be met Francesco dei Medici and Bianca Capello and her first husband, as well as an anonymous "Cardinal"

—a quartet whom in my book, as I completed and published it, you may find to be rechristened Lorenzo and Hypolita and Pescaro and Cesario.

Francesco dei Medici, let it be remarked, appears likewise in Webster's *The White Devil;* and the indolent second Grand Duke of Tuscany, disguised as a blackamoor, slinks through this play in a blood-dabbled rôle such as would have astounded him beyond rhetoric, one imagines, inasmuch as all the iambics of his hole-and-corner behavior in *The White Devil* were begotten by John Webster's morbid genius upon a notion that Italian history would have been colored far more satisfyingly if Francesco, in return for his sister Isabella's death, had seen fit to contrive the murder, after some fashion acceptably blood-curdling, of the husband who killed her.

It was an æsthetic omission which the playwright has rectified with a fine if unscientific poisoning scene and no thought of veracity.

From out of such rectifyings arose an impediment against putting my own first notion into book form. In dealing with the Medici—or with the Sforza, or with the Baglioni, or with any other noble and sufficiently vicious Italian family—the Jacobean dramatists wrote with a Virginian liberality in regard to facts. They took over into their own idealized and never existent "Italy" the gist of the true

Italian story. They abridged that story improvingly, which seems pardonable. But, in the manner of John Webster, they likewise added to the story, with an approach to the same violence which Shakespeare displayed in misrepresenting Macbeth and Lear and Hamlet, their own vivid and outrageous inventions as to the actions of once actual persons; and to do this does not any longer rank as an affair of course.

In writing about the historically pre-eminent, one is expected, nowadays, to keep within a hailing distance of their recorded motives and exploits; so that, in composing an account of the American Revolution, let us say, not many latter-day writers would depict this war as being caused by the unhallowed passion of my former neighbor in the Northern Neck, Colonel George Washington of Mount Vernon, for Queen Charlotte of England. A Jacobean dramatist would have done this, or its equivalent, without turning a hair; and indeed, if it at all suited his purpose, he would have concluded the play with their marriage.

5

I saw, then, when I began to write, after the form of a Jacobean play, *The King Was in His Counting House,* that for me to handle the Medici with any such freedom as the Jacobean playwrights had exercised was forbidden. Even though I desired not to embellish history with their profusion, but rather to abridge it with their dramatic directness, yet this abridgment would crowd the events of fifty years into an indeterminate, not very long while; and by Draconic appraisers, any such condensing, inasmuch as it bought concision at the cost of chronology, might be called inaccurate.

There remained, even so, another method, in no less good Jacobean standing, by which the Medici or any other once actual Italians could enter into Jacobean "Italy." They had merely to travel under assumed names.

When Cyril Tourneur dramatized the murder of Alessandro dei Medici, I remembered, then Tourneur kept the gist of his story. In *The Revenger's Tragedy*, indeed, Tourneur has retained the entire story so far as go his dramatic needs; and although he has added to this story with a free hand, yet he avoids any outright perverting of the received truth, by changing the name of every person concerned. He has written, in fine, a *roman à clef*.

Well, and Tourneur's device, howsoever naïve, was ample. It would serve nicely enough. It would render me impregnable against pedants, it would make pointless the acute carping of sciolists.

So in dealing with Cosimo dei Medici and his familiary concerns, I elected to follow after the methods of Cyril Tourneur rather than of Middleton and of Webster. I would abridge and heighten and omit, very much as did every one of the Jacobeans; but I would likewise change the historical names; and in this way, I would evade any possible charge of lax scholarship. I too, in short, would write a *roman à clef*.

Through such prudential considerations did Cosimo dei Medici assume the alias of Ferdinand dei Vetori; his associates were rechristened variously; for concision's sake, Bianca Capello as Hypolita, and Camilla Martelli as Hermia, were made sisters, and in Carneschi three persons were blended into one person; in place of Florence arose San Marco; and the grand-duchy of Tuscany became the kingdom of Melphé.

6

THE completed tale was published, in 1938, to be received amicably enough by most reviewers, and in consequence by their wards, the reading public. Yet nobody, so far as goes my knowledge, identified that so famous chapter of Italian history which I, as it were, had Jacobeanized; and the omission perplexed me, in view of the numerous books devoted to the Medici, as well as a quite sizable library which concerns Bianca Capello, whom, as Hypolita, I had disguised only in name. Nor was it remarked that her putative father, in my story—Lysander of Athens—had made an earlier appearance in the not uncelebrated drama called *A Midsummer Night's Dream.*

In brief, it was to me, rather than to history, that credit came for having invented, in my latest "ironic romance," the excellent plot of *The King Was in His Counting House.* "Excellent" I am forced here to term it out of deference to my superiors' judgment, which has led dozens of foreign men of letters to find this tale amply worth a retelling. So I too borrowed this handsome story; and my chief error in recasting it took form as a failure to foresee that, to the consumers and connoisseurs of our land's reading-matter, the affairs of sixteenth-century Italy would prove unknown. Much knowledge as to such matters is not, after all, among the demands of the Decalogue, nor does the Talmud teach us concerning such matters.

7

NEXT I began to write out the story of *The First Gentleman of America;* and soon bogged among difficulties. What then impressed me was the unparalleled career of the first native Virginian to enter into history, as a prince among the élite of

Europe; and I needed, so I thought, to embellish this career with a love story. Whereupon the entire affair became intractable, because Don Luis de Velasco appeared stoically to decline any part in the most gaily embroidered and captivating amours which my rebuffed fancy could contrive for my erstwhile neighbor in the Northern Neck of Virginia.

I had approached him, I found, from the wrong angle; I was discoloring a story about which he knew far more than I did; and he seemed to resent my officiousness. So I destroyed that which I had written; and I put aside Don Luis to be wheedled later, it might be, into a cast of mind rather more communicative.

8

WITH *Hamlet Had an Uncle* all seemed clear sailing. My plan here was to retell the Belleforest version of Hamlet's story, which Shakespeare, during the process of reconstructing it into an effective stage play, has so remarkably muddled up as a story; but to recast its style into something as near resembling the style of the sagas from which Belleforest derived as I could manage; and to make of Hamlet's maternal uncle Wiglerus (who in the Belleforest story is hardly more than a name) my protagonist.

One needed here to prune and there to expand, of

course, and one needed to explain to the reader three
Danish laws of the period about which, for all
that they shaped Hamlet's life, Belleforest seems
ignorant; but for any outright invention, so far as
Hamlet was involved, one found no occasion. I was
editing an episode of history, an episode in which
all the major facts about Prince Hamlet of Jutland
were known and could not be changed; whereas the
general manner of my writing was predetermined
by, and molded upon, old Scandinavian sagas. And
so, in the construction of *Hamlet Had an Uncle,* an
historian met with no special difficulty.

This episode from the annals of Denmark, when
it appeared in 1940, was received with a charity
which fostered my hope, and which builded a confirming buttress to my faith, that history must remain forever, as Napoleon put it, a fiction agreed
upon—and agreed upon, moreover, in defiance of
any recorded facts such as may not fit in with this
fiction.

I mean that, in looking over the reviews of this
book, I find them almost wholly divided into two
classes: those which accredit me with having written
an "ironic romance" to burlesque the *Hamlet* of
Shakespeare; and those which, with a noble indignation, point out that if indeed, "as Mr. Cabell alleges,"
or 'as Cabell pretends," at any time before Shakespeare produced his drama, any such upstarts as

Belleforest and Saxo Grammaticus, and a few dozen other annalists, were so presumptuous as to write about Hamlet, then every one of them misrepresented the true story.

One champion of historical veracity, for example, points out that this pseudo-Hamlet does not resemble the actual Hamlet so far as even once during all his lifetime to converse with his father's ghost. And another virtuoso, in dealing (as I must record, quite affably) with "this antique of Mr. Cabell's own devising," has none the less found the introduction of Hamlet into any such barbaric chronicle to be an act of irreverence, because "by the love and wonder and study of thousands, Hamlet and all that concerns him have gained to a kind of divinity." Even in my own home town, the finer sensibilities of Richmond's leading Scandinavian scholar, Mrs. Mable Gieberich, were upset all over the place, in the columns of the *Times-Dispatch*, by the historical inaccuracy of "a Hamlet without a ghost, a Hamlet who is no hero, and [who is] a prince, but not of Denmark."

9

I MIGHT multiply such quotations were it not for my peace-loving nature, and a sedative recollection of how very often I too, in my time, have blundered.

So I remark only that pre-eminent authorities upon reading-matter displayed a sturdy conviction that Shakespeare's story of Hamlet was the authentic original version; and that if, throughout some six centuries before Shakespeare's birth, any other sort of Hamlet had been so ill-advised as to figure in Denmark's annals, why, the less said about it, the better.

Even in the scholastic *Saturday Review of Literature,* one of our most erudite literary critics, Mr. Basil Davenport, after observing that my narrative was "a retelling of *The Hystorie of Hamblet,*" at once equivocated in a proper-minded if inventive support of Shakespeare's monopoly so far as to describe *The Hystorie of Hamblet* as being "that translation from Belleforest which causes scholars to dispute whether it was derived from Shakespeare's play, or Shakespeare's play from it."

Inasmuch as this learned causerie, to the extent that I figured in it, was pleasant-spoken enough, I find my present need ungracious, here to revive this statement. Altruism alone forces me to deplore that in America's foremost publication devoted to what we accept tolerantly as our literature any sort of error can be printed and allowed to pass unchallenged.

—For that Shakespeare in writing *The Tragedy of Hamlet, Prince of Denmark,* made use of the Belleforest *nouvelle,* either in its French or English form, appears likely and, indeed, certain. To the other side, the Belleforest story was printed in 1570. For this reason, except only among our more imaginative literary critics, not very many scholars have seen fit "to dispute whether it was derived from Shakespeare's play," in view of the improbability that at six years old, Shakespeare had as yet published, or had even completed, his masterwork.

10

I MUST add also that when this book appeared in Great Britain it was reviewed by persons who knew more or less about François de Belleforest and about Hamlet's niche in the history of Denmark; so that Shakespeare's own countrymen did not insist that Shakespeare invented Hamlet. No patriot need pretend to admire the English beyond any such extravagancy as statesmen may insist upon; yet their culture is less flimsy than ours; nor do they so far share in our more lofty standards (one notes with regret) as to believe that naïve indignation is an always acceptable substitute for common-sense and an impervious cloaking for ignorance.

So then did it happen that the episode from Danish history, which I had published along with a complete acknowledgment of its derivation, was received in America, by and large, as a not discreditable "ironic romance" which I had invented along with all my "sources."

11

WHEN I returned to Don Luis de Velasco, our parley was arranged upon new terms; for I could see now that the point of his story was the relationship—half affection, half enmity—between the Indian Prince and Don Pedro Menéndez de Avilés. Don Luis' career in Europe, out of which at outset I had planned to make the main part of my book, dwindled into a brief chapter. I had no call to invent for him fictitious amours, nor indeed to invent anything of large consequence. That I would follow contemporaneous annals, and improvise nothing more than seemed needed to fill in the gaps between recorded facts with a cement of not illogical inference, had become the resolve which in writing *The First Gentleman of America*, I obeyed to the reach of my powers.

About the quaint fate of this episode from Virginian history I have spoken at sufficient length in another place. I enjoyed this kindly if grotesque reception, nor did I resent viciously the small amount of money it earned for me. My point here is merely that, yet again, my story was received as having been invented, in its every paragraph, by me. My bibliography of the historical works from which I had borrowed the story of Don Luis de Velasco was dismissed tacitly; and I was granted some undeserved credit for having made up, out of the whole cloth, a fair enough sample of "ironic romance."

12

IT FOLLOWS that as concerns this special trilogy I have not any grievance. No reasonable person, my judgment tells me, ought to complain over having been commended generally, and even in a modest way rewarded, for the display of an inventiveness which he, it so happened, had not displayed; or can very graciously deplore the inextensive literacy of the United States of America as a nation after having profited by it upon three occasions hand running.

Yet furthermore: the apposite and consoling moral of my failure as an historian (I submit) would seem to be that, not merely in the State of Virginia, but in many yet other quarters, most history needs to be accepted as a result of popular election rather than of crude casual facts. I infer likewise that in any and all countries our Virginian method of reforming charitably the past for its own good may be by long odds the most remunerative.

Part Five ε❧

MR. RITCHIE'S RICHMOND

In the early Colonial period [of Virginia] the struggle for existence precluded authorship. Emphasis was placed on statesmanship and forensics to the exclusion of imaginative writing. Following the establishment of the republic, to which the Virginia intelligentsia gave its best thought, the sectional strife of the Fiery Epoch produced statesmen and orators rather than creative writers. The speeches of Patrick Henry and of George Washington, James Madison's FEDERALIST PAPERS, *and everything penned by Thomas Jefferson, rank in clarity, force, and purity of English among the literary monuments of America.*

VIRGINIA: A GUIDE TO THE OLD
DOMINION (*1940*)

1

WITH an aptness which appears always to rest
within the control of malice, the influence of the
Commonwealth of Virginia in American art has
been likened, by a Northern commentator, to the
influence of a serpent—but only, as one makes haste
to add, the influence of a serpent in Iceland. Just as
there were not any snakes in Iceland, so in Virginia,
for decade after decade, did none find, in any arena
of the polite arts, a practitioner whose output it was
possible, through even the most obstinate alliance
of good-will with flattery, to describe as mediocre.

So long as one remembers, it has been the fashion,
in Virginia, to extenuate this prolonged barrenness
of Virginia's culture with the explanation that all the
more highly gifted products of England's first colony
have turned, as a matter of course, toward statesmanship or else have launched forth, upon seas of
upturned faces, as unparalleled orators, because of
each branch of bamboozling's more large emolu-
ments in the form of applause and income. Virginians, in brief, did not elect to excel in the polite
arts, because these arts did not pay; such, rather
more exaltedly worded, has been our excuse.

Purely mercenary considerations, one is thus

urged to infer, prevented His Excellency General
Washington, during hard-earned hours of leisure,
after having achieved his dignified quest to imbed
matrimonially an heiress, from jotting down a few
oratorios; or kept my yet other famous late neighbor, James Monroe, from inditing (in addition to
a Doctrine of which foreigners have been so un-
critical as to accept in its complete form) an autoch-
thonous and more genteel *Iliad;* or delayed Patrick Henry from quite finishing those immortal
paintings upon the superiority of which to many of
the masterpieces of John Trumbull it might be time-
wasting to dwell.

2

Now, for one, I question this habit of explaining the
Mother of Presidents' inability to conceive anything
more permanent than eight items in the, upon the
whole, deplorable list of our Chief Executives. I regret the inevitable inference that the main objective
of an intelligent Virginian must be to increase his
bank account by all means not of necessity exposed
to punishment by the criminal code of Virginia. I
prefer to believe it was not the sordid nature of all
my late great neighbors, such as George Washington and James Monroe and James Madison and
Robert Edward Lee, or even of Don Luis de Velasco,

which prevented any one of them from becoming a world-famous practitioner of this or the other branch of art, and from adding in this way to the glories of the Northern Neck the one glory lacking.

I elect to think that the inferiority, or, to speak with justice, the non-existence of Virginian art for so long a while after Captain Christopher Newport settled Jamestown ought not to be attributed, as a glib matter of course, to the ingrained self-seeking of all native-born Virginians. I protest, rather, that among Virginians, and even in the statuesque bosoms of the more profitably celebrated Virginians, there may have lurked remnants of magnanimity. I believe, in brief, that for our backwardness in matters of art, we of Virginia may have been giving, to the lower world outside the Old Dominion, an explanation not wholly correct.

3

ALL these reflections were the immediate fruitage of a couple of sentences in Agnes M. Bondurant's *Poe's Richmond*, a book which I would recommend very heartily to anyone who takes interest either in Edgar Allan Poe or in the social evolution of Virginia. With literary criticism Miss Bondurant is not concerned; but of the Richmond which Poe knew, the Richmond of the first half of the last century, her portrait is complete and vigorous and salutary.

Two sentences, I said: for Miss Bondurant has recorded, in her description of Richmond's cultural life, as it flickered upon Colonel William Byrd's former "Land at the Falls of James River" a good hundred years ago, this friendly proviso against any reader's possible error:

"It was not the planters"—that is, the landed aristocracy of Virginia—"but the professional and business men of Richmond who were responsible for the promotion of literary culture in the city. These were the people who showed enough appreciation for Dickens and Thackeray to give them pleasant receptions."

Neither one of these sentences—I believe, upon mature deliberation—is intended to be devastating. I would very much like to acclaim Miss Bondurant as a virtuosa of irony, in view of that really unimprovable second sentence; yet after reading her book, I imagine she wrote every word of this sentence without any unladylike indulgence in fiendish cacklings. She perhaps did not even smile.

4

YET I need to point out, in the cause of historical truth, that when Charles Dickens visited Richmond he was not the target of "a pleasant reception." Instead, the professional and business men who were responsible for the promotion of culture in the city of Richmond arranged in his honor, at the Exchange Hotel, "a *petite souper*." He was thus privileged to meet about ninety of the leading commission merchants and tobacconists of Richmond, as well as a Judge of the Supreme Court and a State Senator, at this *petite souper*. That his books were liked by their wives and daughters, they all assured him in the most friendly manner. They themselves did not have much time for reading, it was admitted; but they looked forward, with an unanimous eagerness, to reading several of his books next summer, at the Springs, when one would have leisure for novels. That at least one patron of culture told him, beamingly, how much the speaker had enjoyed Mr. Dickens' *Last Days of Pompeii* appears certain.

Nor need I tell you (I trust) that, as a matter of course, the overseeing of this cultural promotion had been entrusted to a scion of the Northern Neck of Virginia; for in point of fact, it had not been.

Nevertheless, Mr. Thomas Ritchie had passed his boyhood in Tappahannock (when it was yet called by his elders Hobbs Hole), from which county seat he could enjoy, every day, a Pisgah vision of two or more miles of the Northern Neck immediately across the wide Rappahannock River. By means of the public ferry he could, as he did, very often visit the Northern Neck during the formative years of his youth; and thus, its influence had (no doubt) colored the character of Mr. Ritchie, and (perhaps) lent to his oratory that elegance for which in later life he became noted throughout all Richmond. As a toastmaster he ranked without any peer in Richmond.

So then did it come about that Mr. Thomas Ritchie, now the main owner and semi-retired editor of the *Richmond Enquirer*, presided, in his very best toastmasterful manner, over what he described afterward, in his paper, as "this elegant and *recherché* entertainment." At this *petite souper*, Mr. Ritchie commended Mr. Dickens for having passed over the great, the glaring, the magnificent, in order to bring out humble worth and unpretending merit; and for having sought the violet, in its lowly bed, so as to give its perfume to the light of day. The excursive imagination of our young but distinguished guest (Mr. Ritchie stated) had wandered over the whole surface of human nature; yet instead of investing wealth or power with additional attractions, it had seized upon humble points in the human landscape; had lighted them up with the fire of his genius; and had thus given to them that conspicuous position to which they were entitled.

Continuing in Mr. Ritchie's self-admitted task, "to see to it that the circling hours may glide on, gladdening and rejoicing, until after midnight," Mr. Ritchie regretted that "we bring around our distinguished guest no boast of literary circle. We have no Washington Irving to grace the chair; we have no Bryant present to celebrate his praises in rapturous strains."

Then Mr. Ritchie—in perfectly correct present-day form, but more than a hundred years ago, in the March of 1842—went on to explain that this was simply because "the *forte* of the Old Dominion is to be found in the masculine production of her statesmen, her Washington, her Jefferson, and her Madison, who have never indulged in works of imagination, in the charms of romance, or in the mere beauties of the *belles lettres*."

The exact trick of it, one notes, lies in that "mere."

In this manner did the professional and business men who were responsible for the promotion of literary culture in Richmond honor conscientiously the large sales of Mr. Dickens' books, at an elegant and *recherché* entertainment. They were not pleased when, later in the same year, he published his *American Notes*. "Mr. Dickens," the *Southern Literary Messenger* declared, in Richmond's behalf, "was feasted, toasted, and almost worshiped. His laughing at our manners, and ungratefully sneering at our well-meant attentions, has . . . proved a littleness of spirit and that Mr. Dickens is a low-bred man."

5

—THE naming of which magazine reminds me that, while upon his way from New York to Richmond, young Mr. Dickens had granted a pair of interviews to another, but all-negligible, young man of letters who, some five years earlier, had left Richmond rather than starve in Richmond. And just what (at the United States Hotel, upon Chestnut Street, in Philadelphia) Mr. E. A. Poe then remarked as to Richmond stays beyond guessing.

In one mood, he would have described the city as a ghoulish latrine which was kept malodorous by its clientele's hourly discharges of scoundrelism, of vainglory, of stupidity, of scandal, of mutual envy, and of humbug. In another mood, Richmond would have loomed more handsomely, as an Aidenn, the main part of which, along with large portions of the adjoining city of Manchester, happened to be Mr. Poe's ancestral estate, to which by-and-by he must be returning, as a matter of *noblesse oblige,* so as to resume his leadership of the *haut ton.* His special mood throughout these two interviews has remained, regrettably, a detail unjotted down by history's scatterbrained muse.

Clio records merely (through a proper feminine preoccupation with the sartorial) that during the second of these private audiences Mr. Dickens sported a new necktie, somewhat piercingly green, which was held knotted by a necessarily extra-large diamond ring; and that he wore also, under an orange colored dressing gown quilted with violet facings, a red velvet waistcoat which was adorned with two watch chains and a bare half-dozen or so of Mr. Dickens' fine cameo watch fobs, scarcely a pound's weight in all. Thus clad, a benignant monarch of English letters admitted that he had glanced through—why, but yes, to be sure, through *Tales of the Grotesque and Arabesque*—with considerable interest.

He was properly grateful to Mr. Doe for the gift of both volumes; and he believed that one might perhaps arrange to have the book published in England, if Mr. Low really thought the arrangement to be desirable. It seemed only fair, of course, to point out to Mr. Roe that, in the present literary market, a book by an unknown author—and especially, a book of short stories— However! Mr. Dickens would very gladly look into the matter, immediately after his return to England.

He became more hearty. His demeanor implied that he meant to run straightway from the ship dock into the offices of Chapman and Hall, brandishing both volumes, now that Mr. Dickens arose halfway from out of his armchair. He coughed then; he looked at his watch; and Mr. Dickens in this manner got rid of the gaunt, sallow-skinned, fidgeting, abject and yet boastful poor devil who (in threadbare but very neatly brushed clothes, and wearing obviously re-mended rusty gloves) was now wasting yet more of Mr. Dickens' time with some rigmarole or another about the Virginian city of Richmond.

It follows that Clio does not record anywhere what Mr. Poe said to Mr. Dickens as to the Richmond which had declined to honor the genius of Edgar Allan Poe, and in which Mr. Thomas Ritchie ranked as an approved cultural mentor.

6

Poe, let it be repeated, left a city whose culture and whose social life as a whole were dominated by its leading tobacconists and commission merchants rather than starve in Richmond. Throughout Poe's life, Richmond quite steadfastly declined to accept as a desirable citizen the supreme, if not indeed the only, literary genius then alive in the United States.

Here, surely, is conduct upon the part of Richmond which calls for reprehension.

And so, even in Richmond, we who can enjoy nowadays the products of Poe's genius without being concerned with his personality do reprehend Richmond. We dwell, with an appropriate scorn, upon the smug Pharisaic obtuseness of Mr. Thomas Ritchie, and of a bourgeoisie which we are but too liable to miscall as "of his ilk," in regretting that a city which had exiled Poe could not boast of a Washington Irving or a William Cullen Bryant. We remark feelingly upon Virginia's customary neglect of genius until a while after any possible tribute needs take the form of a tombstone; and in contrite Richmond we have gone so far as to erect, but not to support afterward, an Edgar Allan Poe Shrine as a just symbol of our civic remorse.

We omit only, in brief, from our diatribes against Mr. Ritchie's Richmond, to observe that in this special instance Richmond was right. Poe was not a desirable citizen.

7

NOR even as a writer had his career in Richmond seemed edifying. He returned to the home of his boyhood, it may be recalled, in the August of 1835, to become editor of the *Southern Literary Messenger;*

but before the middle of September that which a broad-minded physician called "illness" had compelled Mr. Poe's discharge. He was shipped back to Baltimore and to the debatable solace of his secret marriage with a half-witted child, who reached during this same September her thirteenth birthday. Under a proviso as to his future entire sobriety, Mr. Poe was re-engaged by the *Messenger* in October.

To its pages he contributed, during the year 1836, revamped versions of three stories and of six poems, which in their earlier form he had printed elsewhere; four essays which resembled the majority of his essays in unimportance; that which, to the rational business world of Richmond, appeared to be a pointless and tedious hodgepodge of hocus-pocus, calling it *The Narrative of Arthur Gordon Pym;* and yet another hodgepodge headed "Pinakidia," which, although presented as an original work, turned out to be a batch of quotations from more ancient writers. Here was not much to incite enthusiasm, and nothing at all to arouse in the frilled breasts of Richmond's leading tobacconists any least suspicion that (if it mattered) their city now harbored a literary genius.

Meanwhile, Mr. Poe did, it is certain, increase the circulation of the *Southern Literary Messenger* (even from 700 to 5500 copies a month, by the unreliable testimony of his own figures) through publishing some eighty-odd reviews, for the most part scurrilous, of books which, almost without any exception, were not worth noticing; and of which nowadays only the titles survive. Outside Richmond it was as a book reviewer that Poe gained attention, during his editorship of the *Messenger*, by his forthright mud-slinging at all targets which offered; since in this manner the literati of the republic were compelled for the first time to notice Mr. Poe, upon very much the same principles which would have urged them to notice a rattlesnake. Not many of the city's leading commission merchants, however, were literati.

And meanwhile also Mr. Poe was to be seen, more and more often, during office hours, upon lower Main Street and upon Bank Street, in a condition which toward midnight at earliest might have been found barely pardonable. His periods of recuperation in bed had so lengthened that his virulence in the *Messenger* now dwindled in volume, and began to enrage fewer and yet fewer readers, because of his inability, during these seasons of collapse, to write anything at all. Even in the unexigent part of a public scold he became, in fine, unreliable; and in consequence, the *Southern Literary Messenger* found it a wise stroke of business to discharge Mr. Poe, yet again, and forever, in the December of 1836.

8

SUCH then was the brief editorial career in Richmond which had failed to arouse Mr. Thomas Ritchie's admiring attention. It is true that the leading commission merchants and tobacconists, and perhaps even some few of the circuit judges and state senators of this era, did not regard any current magazine with the enthusiasm of an advertising agent. Yet it was not as an author that Poe failed to meet Richmond's requirements most obviously. In a society where all gentlemen drank pretty heavily as a matter of course, and as a matter of good form abstained from intoxication, he left the demands of good form unhonored. He was found shifty about money. He lied rather too freely; and he had the misfortune, almost invariably, to be detected.

—For Poe, it must be remembered, during this stay of some fifteen months in Richmond, misapplied his attenuated if steel-like powers of invention, all but daily, through misrepresenting the date of his marriage, his wife's age, his income, his heroic past, his ancestry, his erudition, his foster father, his mother-in-law's private fortunes, his life-long record as a rigid teetotaler, and most of his fellow-writers (both *seriatim et en masse,* as Poe's scholarship might well have phrased it) and every one of his employers. He touched virtually no topic which he did not leave smudged with untruth. Yet almost always he improvised under the disadvantage that—in companionable, small Richmond, where the private affairs of very few persons remained unknown to everybody else—his hearers knew he was lying.

And moreover, Mr. Poe's manner was morose and flighty and aloof. He had not the social graces. He was quarrelsome, which was a gentleman's privilege; but always afterward (as male Richmond noted shruggingly) he contrived, somehow, to wriggle out of the duel which, for a gentleman, would have been a fair quarrel's fair epilogue. In brief, Richmond, without any particular violence, disapproved of young Mr. Poe because he did not adhere to a code customary among the well-bred. He was, in a word—a word which, throughout Virginia, still remains all-damnifying, without having any precise definition—"tacky."

So Richmond ignored, at first, this unpleasing personality, and by-and-by its possessor's existence. One may be wholly certain that when Mr. Ritchie, speaking without anguish, commented upon the paucity of fine writers in and about the dining room of the Exchange Hotel, he was not thinking about Edgar Allan Poe either one way or the other. Young Mr. Poe was beyond the consideration of Richmond's élite, in any and all capacities.

9

I PAUSE here to observe that after a lifelong acquaintance with the word "tacky," not until a short while ago did I discover that all dictionaries appear to define this adjective as an "American colloquialism" for "shabby" or "unkempt." Even that Thesaurus which hitherto I had regarded with a misplaced confidence I found to list "tacky (*colloq. or slang*)" between "far-gone" and "decayed."

And it was a grave shock to me to be reading any such wild nonsense; for in Virginia a tacky person is one who, so nearly as I can phrase his deficiency, does not quite know just how to behave in the way that well-born Virginians tacitly expect an equal to behave in civilized intercourse. His appearance may be immaculate, nay, even sumptuous, and his heart a vast ingot of unsullied gold; his shrewdness may loom illimitably against a commensurate background of wealth and of power in the synagogues of business life or of politics; and yet, if he does not know, by sheer intuition, that unworded code which is customary among the indigent, well-bred inner circles of Virginia, why then he remains forever tacky; and no published books upon social etiquette can provide for him aid. —Nor for that matter, I imagine, does there exist any known inanimate object which is more tacky than a book of etiquette, according to our better Virginian standards. It is the sort of bibelot which we are resigned to admire in the drawing-rooms of North Carolina and of Texas. . . .

But I desist. This, after all, is not meant to be a treatise upon linguistics, nor upon shrill interstate bickerings either. I observe merely that in Virginia there is no word more significant, or more deadly, than is "tacky."

10

FURTHERMORE, I observe that my aforetime neighbor in Tappahannock did not keep his implied promise to stop talking immediately after the circling hours of the eighteenth of March, 1842, had glided to midnight. Throughout all Virginia, Mr. Thomas Ritchie, under one or another alias, is still talking. For a full century, Mr. Ritchie has not ever ceased to account for Virginia's defects "in the mere beauties of the *belles lettres*," as in all other mere arts, by pointing out that "the *forte* of the Old Dominion" is to produce great statesmen and unparalleled orators, even at a period when, to the captious, her current politicians and public speakers might appear undazzling.

Nor have we changed at all, I reflected, now that I speculated as to how many hundreds of times I have listened reverently to Mr. Thomas Ritchie, in that throughout Virginia it is still the professional and business men who have charge of our culture. When the leadership of any formal cultural enterprise falls vacant, it is forthwith entrusted, as an affair of course, to a retired or semi-retired man of business who—in our customary phrase—"has the time and the money to attend to it."

I could think of no plain reason why a college endowed by the state should not be conducted by a retired newspaper publisher—like Mr. Thomas Ritchie,—or a civic symphony association by a retired stockbroker, or a commonwealth's pink, large and costly Museum of Fine Arts by the retired head of a department store. All these phenomena in my day I have witnessed. We might likewise be promoting culture in and about Williamsburg, upon a proper mercantile basis, by having hired out an entire town to be demolished into the back-drop for a retired oil magnate's elegant and *recherché* and daily fancy-dress party, among his pensioners' painstaking parodies of the obsolete. —For how better could culture be disposed of, once and for all, than by somebody who had the time and the money to attend to it?

I at least could not find any definite flaw in this theory's logic. But I did know, just as the world knows, that in practice this theory has not worked.

We all know for how long a while the culture of Virginia, as thus comfortably conducted, has proved to be sterile in every field of æsthetics—except only, as I have suggested elsewhere, in the superb and philanthropic romanticizing of Virginian history and in a free-spirited invention of priorities and relics.

11

Now that I speak of Williamsburg, I remark that one considers with a sort of incredulous awe the record of the College of William and Mary, as being the very oldest of Virginia's cultural institutions.

And I do not mean only that nobody can appraise without reverence the huge roster of those among its alumni who, with a pleasing regularity, have continued to become more or less applauded, alike in political and pedagogic and clerical and military and medical fields, and in all other honorific human activities, ever since William and Mary first opened its class rooms in the remote autumn of 1697. I refer instead to the fact that this college has contrived, somehow, throughout the length of two and a half centuries, to produce, with but one exception, in the lank figure of Thomas Jefferson, no graduate who after leaving Williamsburg became distinguished in any branch of creative art.

The event seems not surprising but miraculous. It defies all granted laws of probability that the name of no fairly well known painter, or musician, or sculptor, or novelist, or poet, or playwright, or prose artist, should adorn the long list of the thousands of persons who have been educated, and elaborately educated, at William and Mary. Yet even in the minor craft of writing short stories this college, until lately, could display only Thomas Jefferson as being noteworthy.

I say "until lately" because, for us of Virginia, at any rate, his once famous brief romance, the Declaration of Independence, is debarred from consideration nowadays, through its ugly and unconcealed tinge of anti-British sentiments. We decline to tolerate a canard which describes our revered kinsmen and unfailing patrons, the people of England, as being "deaf to the voice of justice and of consanguinity."

And besides that, as has been mentioned a while back, at this chapter's beginning, a graduate of William and Mary did write, in the Monroe Doctrine, a peculiar display of moderation and common-sense such as at one time was applauded, and even viewed more or less seriously. Yet I do not imagine that nowadays a proper-minded American citizen could endure hearing, without an immediate resort to lynch law, the repetition of any such out-of-date if not actively seditious propaganda as, "In the wars of the European Powers in matters relating to themselves we have never taken any part, nor does it comport with our policy so to do."

Nor is it at all comfortable, for us of Virginia, to remember that it was a Virginian who, when President of the United States, so far neglected the higher principles of a more advanced code of statesmanship as to declare that, in dealing with the Eastern Hemisphere of this planet, "our policy . . . is, not to interfere with the internal concerns of any of its Powers; to consider the government *de facto* as the legitimate government for us; to cultivate friendly relations with it; and to preserve these relations by a frank, firm and manly policy . . ."

But at this point reflection compels me, because of my sound faith in America's present-day more cosmopolitan outlook, to desist from transcribing the Monroe Doctrine. I have cited enough of it, I trust, to make clear the outmoded heresies among which its author wallowed; and which, in Virginia at any rate, we have learned how to ignore politely, without any comment, after very much the same bland fashion in which we have agreed to dismiss an ill-advised and a regrettably premature white settlement, somewhere in Florida, which was not Anglo-Saxon.

12

AND SO (to go back a little), even so do we touch upon a significant fact; which fact is that in the State of Virginia our professional men and our business men have been always the custodians of our culture. The main, the official, promotion of every humane art has been entrusted, without fail, to this or the other coterie of highly estimable tax-payers in the higher brackets who, despite their many virtues, and for all that they had the time and the money to attend to it, yet happened to know very little, or else precisely nothing, about that special art which was their protégé; and so no more than Samson has art thrived in the hands of the Philistines.

Do you let me assure you that no word of these remarks is meant to asperse Philistia. Its bankers and magnates and college professors and statesmen, and its favorite authors and pastors, I have found to be more congenial than are talented persons, by and large; and its overlords I esteem so devoutly, in their own several fields, that I cannot but dislike to see them popped up, like point-device scarecrows, to supervise alien fields in which—like Mr. Thomas Ritchie—they become unhumorous figures of fun.

One grants gratefully that of late years the preeminence of Gath and Ascalon in Virginia has been rendered rather more hurtless by the increased ease of travel. The young with artistic impulses, I mean, have been able, or perhaps forced, to leave Virginia, somewhat as Poe left Virginia, so as to develop their talents elsewhere; and this they have done, with a number of gratifying results.

Ellen Glasgow, who at first glance might appear an exception to this tonic self-exile, none the less traveled far and often; after reaching maturity she passed the greater part of each year outside the State of Virginia; nor during her youth was she the victim of any formal cultural training as dispensed by Virginian standards. Her primary education—it is an open secret—was an affair over which Ellen Glasgow herself presided, with the assistance of that delectable gentlewoman whom, in the novel not without malice called *Virginia*, Ellen Glasgow has portrayed as Miss Priscilla Batte. The remainder of Ellen Glasgow's education was attained through the noticeably un-Virginian pursuit of omnivorous reading.

I have not any remedy to offer as to Virginia's self-admitted unexcellence "in works of imagination." When a state or a city organizes—in Edith Wharton's agreeable phrase—"to pursue culture in bands, as if it were highly dangerous," why, then the machinery of the resultant organization needs, it is obvious, to be handled by persons who are familiar with the chicane of all organizations. That is logic: it is a deduction acted upon by every state in the Union; and yet, just somehow, this mechanical hunting down of culture does fail, in Virginia at any rate, to produce art of noteworthy importance. It produces, instead, in large numbers, art's patron and apologist, as so very blatantly blended in the, I fear, immortal person of Mr. Thomas Ritchie.

Part Six ₰

ALMOST TOUCHING THE CONFEDERACY

The old plantation system of the South was wrecked and the South impoverished by the long years of struggle. If Lincoln had lived, there is no doubt that the whole problem of reconstruction and bringing the Southern states back into the Union would have been more wisely and sanely handled. Instead, it was clumsily handled, on the whole, by vindictive men who wanted to punish the South more than they wanted a great country.

STEPHEN VINCENT BENÉT

1

ALWAYS afterward it was to seem odd, to look back upon the childhood of that myth which you, during your own childhood, were permitted to witness among those of your elders who defined themselves, without any thought of vainglory, or of being contradicted, as belonging to the best families of Virginia. Like Ulysses before King Alcinous in your *Old Greek Stories Simply Told*, or like Æneas at Carthage in *Stories of Old Rome*, your elders, to every side of you, were engaged in retelling the tragedy in which their own part had not been minor. No more than for young George Washington, in your *Child's History of Virginia*, was it conceivable for anyone of them ever to consider perverting the truth consciously. That they were wholly in earnest as to everything which concerned the sacred Lost Cause for which their lives had been risked, and their fortunes demolished, went equally, as people phrase it, without saying.

So you meant only that, every now and then, you wondered about your elders and the two different ways in which they talked.

The atmosphere of the Richmond of your childhood, to a very marked degree, was elegiac. The Confederacy had fallen, which was bad enough in all conscience; and, which appeared to have been far more horrible, Reconstruction had followed. Herewith one employs the word "horrible" on account of the backwardness of the English language, which, as yet, has not produced any adjective better qualified to express the more lenient aspects of Reconstruction, as your elders viewed Reconstruction. Not until a long while afterward did you have any special notion as to what "Reconstruction" might signify, precisely, because when you first began to remember things you knew only that it had let loose strange monsters, which were called Carpet-baggers; and that these had acted real mean to everybody in Richmond, and over in Petersburg also.

2

WHEN your elders talked about The War they reminded you of those prophets and the several other people in nightgowns who, according to the full-page picture in your *Book of Bible Stories*, had sat down by the rivers of Babylon; nor in later years did you change this opinion, materially. You did not mean that your elders behaved in this way upon the banks of the James River or near the Canal. That was where you went fishing.

Instead, it was before the tall writing desks of

their grandfathers, or between a dignified pitcher of ice water and a flag of the Confederacy on a gold-painted pole, that your elders sat down very solemnly; and they lamented together, in memoirs and upon memorial days, when they remembered their Zion, that South which had been, and which now was at one with Babylon.

They spoke—not without any ardor, nor did they shun the more sturdy graces of elocution—as to a paradise in which they had lived once upon a time, and in which there had been no imperfection, but only beauty and chivalry and contentment. They spoke of womanhood, and of the brightness of hope's rainbow, and of the tomb, and of right upon the scaffold, and of the scroll of fame, and of stars, and of the verdict of posterity. But above all did they speak of a thin line of heroes who had warred for righteousness' sake in vain, and of four years' intrepid battling, even from the McLean farmlands at Bull Run to the McLeans' parlor at Appomattox.

When your elders spoke as to General Robert E. Lee, it was in the tones which other, less fortune-favored nations reserve for divinity, because a god, or at any rate a demigod, had come forth from the Northern Neck of Virginia to dwell in the Confederate States of America; and they who spoke had beheld with their own eyes his serene glory. There was no flaw in it when, upon tall iron-gray Traveller, he had ridden among them, like King Arthur returned from out of Avalon, attended by the resplendent Launcelots and Tristrams and Gareths and Galahads, who, once upon a time, had been the other Confederate generals.

And about yet another sublime and gracious being, who resembled wise Merlin, your elders spoke also, calling him Jefferson Davis, and telling about his downfall, and about his imprisonment in a place which was more discomfortable than Broceliande. All this had happened to Mr. Davis, so you learned gradually, after a great host of very bad people called Yankees, who reminded you of Mordred's "great host" in the last chapter of the book that Uncle Landon gave to you one Christmas, had seized on the fair kingdom which really and truly belonged to General Robert E. Lee.

And still later, those Carpet-baggers had come, right into Richmond. Only they were not at all like big caterpillars or large bugs, it was explained to you. They were much worse.

3

IT WAS confusing, the way in which your elders talked about things which no great while before you were born had happened in Richmond. —Because you lived in Richmond: and Richmond was not like Camelot. Richmond was a modern city, with sidewalks and plumbing and gas light and horse cars.

You could see for yourself that damsels in green kirtles and fire-breathing dragons and champions in bright armor did not go up and down the streets of Richmond, but only some hacks and surreys, and ox-carts hauling tobacco, or it might be a doctor in his buggy, and sometimes a herd of sheep or of cows (which spilled all over the brick sidewalks and had to be shouted at by men with long sticks), or the boys that were bigger than you were, riding most enviably upon tall bicycles; or perhaps it was just the man with a hand bell and a little grindstone in a sort of thin wheelbarrow who sharpened your mother's carving knives and scissors, or the hokey-pokey man, or some colored people that were selling fine fresh vegetables out of their cart, or the organ-grinder with his monkey dressed in unforgettably dusty red velvet.

Anyhow, there were not in Richmond any such old-time things as falchions and guerdons and varlets. Richmond was a progressive and up-to-date city which had re-arisen triumphantly, like a phœnix from out of its ashes, so everybody said. Richmond was not at all like Camelot or Caerleon upon Usk; and so you found it kind of curious that the way in which your elders talked, upon platforms, reminded you of your *Stories of the Days of King Arthur,* by Charles Henry Hanson, with Illustrations by Gustave Doré.

That was a real nice book, you thought at this season. It was a grayish-blue and rather small book. Upon the cover of it was a brickdust-colored picture of Sir Gawaine, with an edifice of curly plumage on top of his helmet, and ostentatiously undulant for a good distance behind it also, as he rode toward the Green Chapel, which "was the most perilous place in the world"; and "this compilation contains"—so did the chapter that was called "Preface" tell you— "an epitome of the Arthurian Legends," in which (as was declared farther on) "no occasional allusions and episodes which make them unfit to be placed in the hands of juvenile readers . . . have been retained."

You liked this book very much. But you could not understand why almost everything that in public your elders said about The War seemed, somehow, to have come out of this book.

4

MOREOVER, you noticed that your elders did not speak in the same way when they were just talking to one another in your father's drugstore, or in your mother's dining-room at Sunday night supper (when everybody ate out of the best plates, which had a different sort of bright colored bird painted upon each one of them), or when your elders were playing whist in the big and high-ceilinged pale-brown back-parlor of your grandfather's house, down upon Governor Street. When, with all eight of the gas jets lighted overhead, in the gleaming copper and crystal-hung chandelier, your elders played whist, pensively and without any excitations, then they used to save time, and avoid argument, by turning up the very last card in the pack so as to find out at once what was going to be trumps. And upon such reflective occasions they would talk differently about The War and the people who had been in it.

They would speak, for instance, of Abraham Lincoln. You recollected afterward that never did you hear them speak, in private, as to Abraham Lincoln with enmity. If your elders had found in his life a great deal which demanded praise, then they must have withstood these demands with success; but his death was regretted—upon grounds that were wholly practical, so you observed later—as having been to the South a misfortune. Had Abraham Lincoln lived, the South would have been dealt with more mercifully and more decently, said your elders. That he was a poor-white and untidy person they said also; he, in short, was tacky: but the man was well-meaning.

Those stories which your elders had heard, and which they repeated urbanely, as to his private life, were rather curious sounding sometimes. You did not understand, for some while to come, what the joke was about in a number of them; and he seemed, too, to have had a lot of fathers.

Yet these anecdotes, if spiced with derision, remained unflavored by malice. Your elders did but laugh—"high and disposedly"—to remember that small-town lawyer whom those Yankees had thought fit to be their President. He, in the opinion of your elders, most certainly was.

That Mr. Lincoln had displayed any element of greatness, was a suspicion which did not occur to your elders. Mr. Lincoln was regretted unresonantly, without raising one's polite soft voice, as a shrewd but not unamiable politician, whose death, which was an ill-advised affair in the manner of its occurrence also, had happened to expose a conquered South to the oppression that he, living, would have opposed. Young Booth, in brief, through the most excellent of motives, had made a tragic blunder. That, so nearly as you could word this matter, during the long years which were to come later, seemed to be the opinion of your elders as to what, in their belief, had been Mr. Lincoln's unfortunate and involuntary importance. They almost always called him "Mr. Lincoln," with formal politeness.

And in the cause of vividness, you came by-and-by to regret this opinion. You would have preferred to record that your elders spoke with a more lively emotion about Abraham Lincoln, either as an heroic enemy or as an abhorred enemy. But in point of fact they did not, because at no time were they much interested in their fallen opponent, as a person, either one way or the other.

"Young Booth, through the most excellent of motives, had made a tragic blunder." Such, one can but repeat, was the verdict of well-bred Virginia as to Abraham Lincoln's murder, at a time when you were still in short trousers and long stockings stragglingly divorced by a neutral zone of chapped flesh. —For John Wilkes Booth had been admired as an actor and liked as a person, immediately before the War Between the States, when for some two years he had figured handsomely, in and about Virginia's capital city, as a member of Mr. Kunkel's Stock Company; Virginia did not know Lincoln except by reports, the most of which were ungrandiose; and moreover, not even the most highly gifted of your elders was able quite to anticipate a re-united republic's final verdict as to the unfortunate commemoration of your birthday a good fourteen years ahead of time. You, it is to be feared, thought, while your elders talked, that the most interesting thing about this sort of mixed-up sounding Mr. Lincoln was, after all, his having been shot on your birthday.

Such memories troubled you, by-and-by, after your knowledge as to Abraham Lincoln's now accepted importance had been enlarged; and you became perturbed when you tried to imagine anyone of your once familiar elders, who had known John Wilkes Booth, as being buttonholed by Mr. Carl Sandburg during Mr. Sandburg's gathering of the needed data for his definitive large Life of Lincoln.

"Sir," Mr. Sandburg would inquire of your boyhood's acquaintance, just as Mr. Sandburg has inquired of the present age, "who was this Booth? What was he like? In what kind of a green-poison pool of brain and personality had the amazing and hideous crime arisen?"

"Why, I can but tell you—" the well-bred Virginian would reply.

"—For out of a mediocre fame and a second-rate reputation as a mimic," Mr. Sandburg would continue, "this Booth has wrapped the letters of his name with a weird infamy synonymous with Enemy of Mankind. His name on a thousand occasions is to go unspoken with loathing for the unspeakable and untouchable; a pitiless, dripping, carnivorous, slathered, subhuman and antihuman beast mingling snake and tiger; the unmentionable; the American

Judas with a brain that was a haunted house of monsters of vanity, of vampires and bats of hallucination."

—To which the Virginian would answer in winged words such as, after reflection, you preferred not to imagine, because in permitting them to pass the barrier of his teeth, he might laugh (also Homerically) on account of some superficial differences between Middle Western rhetoric in anything which concerns Lincoln and the South's rhetoric as to the Confederacy. Yet it seemed to you that instead of laughing he would say, just as he did of old,—

"Young Booth, suh, through the most excellent of motives, made a tragic blunder."

And the Virginian, the unchangeable Virginian of the 1880's, would thus dismiss the entire matter serenely.

5

—For the main business in life of your elders was to create a myth which was not intimately concerned with the perhaps equally great myth of Lincoln, and which in consequence did not need to clash with it. They were creating (so did you decide later), in the same instant that they lamented the Old South's extinction, an Old South which had died proudly at Appomattox without ever having been smirched by the wear and tear of existence. They perverted no facts consciously; but they did omit, from their public utterances or from their printed idyllic narratives, with the tact of a correctly reared person, any such facts as appeared undesirable—without, of course, ever disclaiming these facts.

A gentleman, in brief, does not tell lies. There is no ruling which denies to him a judicious amount of reticence.

So you noticed, for example, when in private your elders talked about him who had reminded you of wise Merlin, that they did not really like this Mr. Jefferson Davis or admire very many of his doings. They stated their reasons, in terms which you found to be incomprehensible and of no large interest, because you were wondering why Mr. Davis appeared to be an entirely different person when people talked about him upon platforms. And some of the more prominent knights of the Confederate Round Table seemed to have been like that also, when, at supper or during those leisured whist games, your elders spoke about them.

Your elders told then of how one of these heroes had been a trifle too drunk to sit upon his horse at any time during the battle which made him famous, and so had not been able to take part in this special battle. And nobody blamed him, of course, for what was really a rather good joke on the strapping daredevil: it was just a bit of bad luck which might have happened to almost anyone. Quite otherwise did your elders discourse as to another illustrious person, who, so they said, had hid in a barn when he ought to have been fighting; and who had been forced, quietly, to get out of Virginia, and to go north, where, in addition to being made a judge, he had become a professional Confederate veteran with a prestige so enormous that it still nurtures his descendants. None envied him these glories; nor did anyone wish to remove his bogus lustre from out of that which, upon platforms, your elders called the eternal roster of fame. It was simply that he could not ever come back to Virginia.

Your elders spoke also as to the final words of a more authentic hero, which, it appeared, were not the soldierly utterance that is set down in every Confederate Arthuriad, but a request for the bedpan; as to with how large thrift yet another pre-eminent idol of the Confederacy had behaved in renting out his renown, for advertising purposes, to a pack of gamblers, year after year; as to the manner in which an out-at-elbows paladin had apostatized in order to become an ambassador; and as to the quaint fury with which a half-dozen or more ex-chieftains of the Lost Cause were now publishing a surplus of in-

convenient candors in their depreciations of one another.

Nor was this by any means all that which your
elders talked about, in their quiet and matter-of-
fact and half amused voices, when they spoke as to
the divinities, and as to the wives of these divinities,
whom in public they worshipped.

To a child, who could not understand that for the
health of human ideals every national myth needs
to be edited and fostered with an unfailing patience,
the discrepancy was puzzling; but you did reason it
out, by-and-by. Your elders were not telling any lies,
either in private or upon memorial days, about their
technically unstained and superhuman heroes, or
at least not exactly. It was just that grown people
told only a part of the truth when they climbed up
on platforms, and did not talk about things which
were not nice, such as getting drunk, or like bed-
pans.

6

AND it seemed to you remarkable, in later years,
that you could not recall hearing your elders talk
about any of the Union generals, except only a very
little bit about a General Sherman, who burned up
houses, and perhaps slightly more than that about
an oddly named General Beast Butler, who appeared

to have stolen some teaspoons. That which your elders said as to "Mr. Lincoln" has been recorded; but they did not talk much about Abraham Lincoln, either. They liked better to talk about their own people. And if constantly they derided Yankees, or if in particular they denounced the wicked doings of Carpet-baggers, yet, as you remembered it afterward, to neither one of these evil races was granted the distinction of surnames. So did they remain to you, at this time, an anonymous and unaccounted-for "great host" such as at Salisbury Plain had destroyed King Arthur.

Your elders, in brief, were not mad with the armies and the leaders of the armies that had invaded and seized upon the fair kingdom which really and truly belonged to General Robert E. Lee. They just kind of made fun of them. They were not even very much interested in those Yankee soldiers who had killed off a lot of your own uncles and cousins. It was only when they talked about Carpet-baggers. Carpet-baggers must have been rather like ogres, or perhaps they were churls and fell caitiffs, you decided. —Because you were getting sort of sleepy. It must be mighty near nine o'clock. Anyhow, whenever grown-up people talked about Carpet-baggers they would get mad as a wet hen.

But that did not last for more than a little while. Pretty soon they would go back to talking, almost as if they were sitting in church instead of right here in your grandfather's back-parlor, about what a real fine place all the South used to be, and Virginia in particular.

7

THEY were making history after a time-approved fashion. Even in the same instant that, westward and northward, about the benign figure of Abraham Lincoln, as the messiah of the United States of America, was being assembled an epitome of legends in which no "occasional allusions and episodes which make them unfit to be placed in the hands of juvenile readers . . . have been retained," just so in Virginia was being edited and amended and enhanced, after the same chaste manner of Charles Henry Hanson, our own epic of the Old South. In both instances, loyalty required of each myth's makers that more or less should be left out, and that an appreciable deal should be recolored, for the good of mankind at large. And in both instances, the reshapers and the editors of these national myths, with the naïve duplicity of all other devout artists in fiction, even while they observed with some human pride how very far they had bettered veracity, yet, in part, believed their romanticizing to be wholly veracious.

You found it difficult to explain, this bifold mood

in which human beings create, as though by instinct, the one sort of history which their descendants can find profitable; and which alone, because of this mood, their descendants do acquire and try to keep faith with. You at least could not ever explain this half-mythopœic and half-critical frame of mind, not quite intelligibly, not even to yourself.

You knew only that, in Richmond, during your childhood, you had seen this dual mood about its beneficent labors. And you knew also, very much as you had observed in talking about the colonizing of Virginia, that for anyone of us to investigate, in the bleak light of common-sense, these two twin noble myths of the Old South's perfection and of Abraham Lincoln's perfection, or to contemn yet any other legend about our forefathers' perfection, to become not unworthy of which a delusion may spur us, would be to repeat the unthrift of prying Ham and of ill-judging Esau, those deficient inheritors.

—For each one of them, as you recalled from afar your long-perished *Book of Bible Stories*, had lost all which rightfully had belonged to him. That meant something rather important, you decided. It meant that for human beings it might be wiser, even at the price of some inconsistency, to maintain the beliefs that were agreeable and inspiring and magnanimous.

159

Part Seven ᘒᕽ

GENERAL LEE OF VIRGINIA

Lee set an animating example of the "antique virtue" of equanimity. That quality is higher than its noblest component, which is courage. Equanimity is the state of mind which submits itself willingly to the judgment of time, in the consciousness of righteous effort and in the humble admission that the finite mind cannot be infallible. This means, in terms less abstract, that Lee believed in the invincibility of character, and thought that the man who had done the best of which he had knowledge could leave the rest to God.

DOUGLAS SOUTHALL FREEMAN

1

WITH all proper deference, Sir, I introduce myself
to your attention as being a grandson of that Dr.
Cabell who, in Richmond, lived next door to you, at
709 East Franklin Street, and with whom you were
medicinally familiar. My father likewise you would
remember, as that Robert Cabell who at the age of
sixteen, as a cadet of the Virginia Military Institute,
took part in the Battle of New Market, where his
elder brother, William, another cadet, then eighteen
years old, was killed.

I present these credentials not in vainglory but
to attest that I, born of your people and of your caste
and of your adherents, was reared among them who
remembered and who spoke of you, in affectionate
rather than in religious terms, as a friend whom one
had treated for rheumatism, or as a neighbor with
whom one conversed, daily and casually, as to household affairs and the current weather. I have heard
even of some personal foibles not at all to my present
purpose beyond the fact that their attested existence
has kept you always, in my thoughts, human.

It has been since infancy my privilege, in brief,
to comprehend that you were not the marmoreal
effigy which, along with Jehovah, the South at large

yet worships as a matter of good form and as a prerequisite for political preferment. That fervently I applaud Virginia's loyal, outrageous romanticizing of Virginia's history and of Virginia's former leaders has been explained. Even so, I incline to distinguish: for about you alone of historic Virginians I have need to think, perforce, in the unglamorous aspect of a not-young next-door neighbor, who was troubled with rheumatism; and because of one or two yet other reasons you appear to me best left untouched by the well-meant titivations of our historians and by the blatant adulations of oratory.

2

I PAUSE here to reflect with gratitude upon the circumstance that I was not honored with your acquaintance. I can imagine no more harrowing experience than to be seated facing you, for the first time, tete-à-tete. You would be courteous, and impressive-looking, and very conscientiously jocular, in dealing with young Bob Cabell's son. You would inquire if I was writing anything nowadays. When I confessed to a book in progress, then you would ask what I was going to call it. You would not pretend, or at least not with precision, that immediately after the concerned book had been published, "its perusal" would become for you an "evening's recreation," as did Philip Stanhope Worsley's translation of the complete *Iliad*, which he dedicated to you. I have sometimes wondered what Mr. Worsley thought about that special form of acknowledgment when connected with an epic poem in twenty-four books.

To me at any rate you would convey merely a vague but genial impression that you meant to read several of my novels, sometime next summer, at Rockbridge Baths or the White Sulphur Springs, when one would have leisure for novels. You would then speak (I very much fear) as to the importance of good literature. You would regret that in Virginia we have perhaps tended somewhat to neglect the production of literature in favor of statesmanship and oratory. You would feel it your duty to admit that as a rule you preferred to read historical books, as being works of truth, rather than novels and romances. —For history, you would add, enables one to get correct views of life and to see the world in its true light. That will help one to live pleasantly; to do good; and when summoned away from living, to leave this world without regret. You would, I think, refer to Shakespeare and Milton as being desirable models for a writer of fiction to keep in mind.

And I, because of my very great reverence for you, I would fidget; and I would try my utmost to get you to talk about some of the hundreds of matters which you understood better than you did literary affairs; and you would still go on and on, like a highly courteous steam-roller, until I was able to effect my escape.

But after that, if only I too lived next door to you, and were thus able to speak with you informally from time to time, without being petrified by the dictates of your amiability and of your conscience, why, we would get on, I believe, fairly well together. —For I once knew a great many of your well-bearded contemporaries among the well-born Virginians to whom it was permitted to survive you. And to say that I found almost every one of these my dignified elders to be dull-minded would be wrong, because the statement, far too flagrantly, would be an understatement. And the true point, after all, is that I found these stately and sedate and large-hearted gentlemen, even in their dull-mindedness, to be wholly admirable.

3

It may please you, Sir, to hear, in the event of this letter's ever reaching you, that nowadays you rank so very highly among the military geniuses of historic record that several Englishmen have been moved to commend your campaigns as being, for an

American, remarkably well executed. The Germans likewise have studied your tactics with profit. All we Virginians, therefore, expatiate concerning your martial exploits, and do not dwell sufficingly, I submit, upon the circumstance that, through defeat, you passed from relative greatness to an unique greatness.

There have been many other talented generals (and among them a fair sprinkling of scoundrels), and with all the more admirable of these you may be compared, variously, so far as went your activities until, and including, the afternoon of the ninth of April, 1865, when at Appomattox Court House you surrendered the Army of Northern Virginia. For your conduct afterward, throughout the five and a half years of living which as yet remained for you, after Appomattox, there is no parallel; and for this reason, we incline, nowadays, to regard your behavior during this same period with a perplexed incredulity, and to say little about it.

Our main difficulty is that although you did not ever utter, in blunt point of fact, your one notable apothegm, to the effect that "duty" is the most sublime word in the English language, yet at every moment, throughout some sixty-three years, you would seem to have been guided by this apothegm. And most upsettingly did this become noticeable after Appomattox.

So are we condemned to read with a stunned amazement as to your unbusinesslike conduct when you were then tendered any number of substantial tributes, ranging from a manor house in England (with an annuity thrown in) to the control of large corporations in New York City, and including the governorship of Virginia as well as command of the Roumanian army and the presidency of the Chesapeake and Ohio Railway. The highly remunerative and purely ornamental offices which were urged upon you by the directors of life insurance companies, from all quarters of the country, would appear to defy computation; and at this period so unrelentingly were you pressed for money in hand that the final acre of your once considerable land holdings had been confiscated for taxes, when the bland charms of so many sinecures implored your acceptance.

Yet every one of these offers, when they thus came to you in shoals, you declined, saying courteously:

"I am grateful; but I have a self-imposed task which I must accomplish. I have led the young men of the South in battle. I have seen many of them die on the field. I shall devote my remaining energies to training young men to do their duty in life."

And with that, you took over the presidency of poverty-stricken and obscure and dilapidated Washington College, in the gaunt hill-town of Lexington,

Virginia, at the gaunt salary of $1500 a year.

In this manner did you dismiss the homage and the amenities which were yours for the taking. You chose instead to become the headmaster of a country boarding school in a mountain village, with four teachers to aid you in the instructing of about fifty pupils. —For this, as you remarked equably, was the one task in civilian life for which your four years' experience as an instructor at West Point had fitted you; and the age-stricken, fallen champion was still resolute, as in a letter to your wife you explained your set purpose, "to accomplish something for the benefit of mankind and the honor of God."

4

HERE is a saying which surprises and which stirs the blood with its naïve nobility and with what I can but term its arrogant meekness. It is a phrase, one feels, which Valiant-for-Truth would have uttered, if only John Bunyan had been so happily inspired as to think of it. And indeed I do not know but that, with a glow of justifiable auctorial pride, Miguel de Cervantes might have ascribed this same phrase to the Knight of La Mancha.

So then, of your own free will and against the protests of common-sense, did you obey those old-world considerations which, in Virginia, our leaders as yet honor between election days, and lay aside the command of an army in order to take up the petty duties of a country schoolmaster. . . .

Now, as a married man, I confess to some wonderment that Mrs. Lee did not, as it were, put her foot down and take a firm stand in this matter. . . . But I dismiss the ignoble thought. I blush to have harbored it, howsoever transiently; and I believe that in a life over-brimming with magnanimities this was your most heroic action. I take this quiet, stubborn putting aside of all self-interest to be admirable beyond wording. And indeed it is an event which, occurring as it does in the so constantly over-colored history of Virginia, quite frankly staggers me, because one does not at all know what to say about it with a proper flamboyance.

—For it did happen, attestedly; it seems to me a most noteworthy happening; and yet by no stretch of the imagination, or through any athletics in the way of rhetoric, can it be made a romantic happening. "On October 2, 1865, in the presence of the trustees, professors and students, after a prayer by the Rev. W. S. White, Robert E. Lee took the oath of office as required by the laws of the College, and was thus legally inaugurated as its president." Not even a Virginian can very well romanticize any proceedings so humdrum.

Nor did you romanticize them. You quite simply and in a wholly matter-of-fact manner did that which seemed right to you, "for the benefit of mankind and the honor of God."

5

It is through this unbending and invincible and even somewhat stolid integrity that you have become divided from the other leaders in the War Between the States, upon both sides; for to no one of them, upon either side, was a judicious amount of compromise and of self-advancement wholly unknown—after, at any rate, the war had ended. Each one of them then did, in one way or another, make use of his famousness as an asset which, to phrase the affair bluntly, he cashed in at the best market value obtainable.

There was no blame involved. Such was, and such remains, the customary practice of all leaders after all wars. But you, with an heroic obtuseness, did not know how to compromise; and you went to what we, your successors and your inferiors in the present-day State of Virginia, cannot but regard as somewhat fantastic lengths, in order to prevent your celebrity from becoming a source of income.

You thus seem to move among your contemporaries, if not quite as a perceptible un-Puckish changeling, at least like a foreigner; and I imagine that, just somehow, an elderly Roman of the Republic may have wandered into the middle of the nineteenth century. I then check these irresponsible fancies. I resolve to be the one Southerner who does not babble about you balderdash. You were but human, I remind myself; you developed during the latter years of your life an embarrassing habit about which rumor yet whispers; one has heard likewise that your last words required to be edited; my own grandfather used to solace your undignified groanings when you had rheumatism; and if only Mary Custis Lee had combined a quiet, quite firm stand with a few frozen observations as to what already she had put up with, over and yet over again, why, then you would have surrendered, I imagine, like most other husbands.

6

EVEN so, Sir, I cannot avoid remarking the un-Christian and beneficent manner in which you denied to your final years that customary solace of the retired warrior, alike in victory and defeat, of producing his memoirs, in which to expose unflinchingly their writer's grandeur of soul, and to acknowledge with a manly regret the stupidity and the viciousness of his competitors and adversaries.

That you did come rather perilously close to writing a book about the War Between the States, there is no denying. Even upon the sheer brink of bespotting in this way your unique glory with printers' ink did you pause during the latter half of 1865, when temporarily you had been divorced from discretion by a desire "that the bravery and devotion of the Army of Northern Virginia [may] be correctly transmitted to posterity." And one flinches to conjecture what would have been the result if you had addressed toward posterity at large that amicably heavy-handed instructiveness which was far better reserved for the tiny classrooms of Washington College.

But accident, or your infirm health, or the lack of authentic data, or else (as one very much prefers to think) those unlimited funds of common-sense such as you displayed always in dealing with any matter which did not threaten to beget your self-advancement, adverted you from blundering into the barren, and dreary, and the necessarily forever dubious, verbose quagmires of self-justification and of special pleading into which, a while later, floundered Jefferson Davis and most of the other surviving overlords of the Lost Cause and——how far more calamitously!——the shrill widows of them who had not survived.

Here I am tempted. I am moved to speak as to that

loud locust-plague of deplorable volumes emanating from the households of your former generals and army chaplains which, during the late 1860's and throughout the next twenty-five years or thereabouts, in attempting to belaud the Confederacy, so very nearly succeeded, through their writers' naïve egotism and their mutual jealousy, in convincing mankind in general that the Confederacy must have been organized and controlled by the mentally handicapped.

But instead of being thus foolhardy, I prefer to borrow, very cautiously, from my adroit, sage friend, Douglas Freeman, the reserved statement, "Perhaps it is well that General Lee did not write his memorial of his Army."

7

I, TO the other side—as being not quite an author who regards the income fetched by his books with an indifference wholly glacial,—I cannot but marvel over the opportunities which, hereabouts also, you ignored, in the approved manner of Virginia, politely, without any comment. If you had written your memoirs, or had you connived in a stratagem not unknown among military circles, of merely signing your memoirs, you overnight would have become affluent.

As Stephen Benét has remarked, "Every Southern family would have bought that book, if it had to starve to do so." And very nearly every Northern family would have purchased it likewise, because of somewhat different motives, during those late 1860's, when you remained—as with an immortal mildness you acknowledged the ever recurrent demand for your imprisonment and execution—"an object of censure to a portion of the country."

Nor would your book's foreign sales have been less than unprecedented. Like Mrs. Calvin Ellis Stowe, your contemporary, who, under the regrettable influence of intuition, wrote, in Brunswick, Maine, a book devoted for the most part to life in an unvisited Louisiana—that very famous treatise which she called *Uncle Tom's Cabin*, and to which you beyond doubt must have accorded "a perusal,"—you also might have flourished in every known language which ranks, alphabetically, between the Armenian and the Wallachian. And you refused, you refused with an equable and courteous finality, thus to flourish.

You had reached late middle life. Your health had failed. You were, like all other Virginians then living in Virginia, as poor as that perhaps fabulous fowl to which Virginians refer, without any specified Biblical warrant, as "Job's blue turkey hen." The world awaited your memoirs. Many publishers

pleaded for your memoirs. You had merely to au-
thorize the appearance of your memoirs in order to
ensure your life's future material welfare. You did
not even have to be at pains to write your memoirs;
for hundreds upon hundreds of your loyal adorers
would have performed for you this taskwork with a
delighted gratitude. Your name would sell the results; but you were not willing to sell your name.

8

DAILY, during those bitter years when Carpet-baggers reigned in Virginia, you thus faced with a polite
stubbornness the same temptings which had wooed
your former neighbor in the Northern Neck, Don
Luis de Velasco, some three hundred years earlier.
—For like him, in order to win affluence and applause and every other agreeability of life, you had
merely to do nothing. You had only not to thrust
away that which your circumstances now proffered
to you with a devoted and incessant profusion.

Yet like the first known of all Virginians, you declined to be pampered by fortune. Like him, you
hard-headedly preferred to sacrifice, to your own
ideas about honor, your private welfare; and the
incentives which had led him to contrive a massacre
thus made of you a schoolteacher.

So then did it fall about that, always with a

courteous but unshaken finality, you refused to accept any benefits whatever which were offered to you because of your part in the War Between the States, a war in which always your part had been, quite simply and quite explicitly, and indeed with a sort of prosaic humbleness, to defend the rights of your mother state against violation. A gentleman, so you quietly contended, does not either expect or take a reward for having attempted to save his mother from being raped.

A creed so improvident was not universal in your own day, and it has become so much more or less incomprehensible, to our later times, that even your most sympathetic biographers still cast about for some further motives to prompt you. But I do not think that any common-sense motives were needed, so far as went your decision in a matter which touched your sense of honor; and to purvey them through guesswork seems rather like suggesting that a son in defending his mother may have been actuated, yet furthermore, by his belief that the assailant had a venereal disease.

9

THAT I begin to speak with magniloquence, and become a prey to the illogic of lofty emotions, I observe with discomfort. Very vainly, through a desire to be

the one Southerner who does not babble about you
balderdash, had I resolved to address you with your
own equanimity. It cannot be done—or at least not
by any Virginian. And so, when I attempt to think
about you as you appeared in the body, and to appraise you as being a conscientious and somewhat
ponderous, quiet-spoken and gray-bearded and
stoop-shouldered Confederate veteran, such as in my
youth I knew by scores, the affair does not come off.
—For my blood warms to you, betrayingly; and reason, defeated by atavism, quits the field.

You were General Lee; you might have done this,
that, or the other, it may be, with more wisdom or
with a larger profit; but there is no living Virginian
who can convince himself of the possibility. We prefer instead to revere you; should your career reveal
any mistakes or shortcomings, why, then we stand
ready to revere them also; for in remembering you,
we believe, with a loyalty which we of Virginia do
not accord to any other person, "that the man who
had done the best of which he had knowledge could
leave the rest to God." Nor in the event of an unfavorable decision, is it with Jehovah, Sir, that your
people would be siding.

Part Eight ॐ

IS OF SOUTHERN LADIES

TO LOUISA NELSON

*"At me ab amore tuo diducet
nulla senectus."*

THE CREAM OF THE JEST

1

THAT, without any fear of succeeding, the intrepid native Virginian will dauntlessly attempt to conceal his superiority to everybody else, remains a tribal virtue which has not escaped the comment of anthropologists. He treads among the commonalty of other commonwealths, it has been remarked, with the meticulous and maddening courtesy of M. le Duc upon a casual visit to the peasantry of this or the other of his minor estates. And yet not really for this Virginian version of politeness is any living Virginian who, let us say, can remember when Grover Cleveland occupied the White House at all blameworthy. Rather is this an enforced trait which has been developed in the man's nature by two circumstances such as through no precautions could he have avoided.

The one circumstance is that throughout the first years of his life (during which his character was taking form, irretrievably) he was reared as a godling who could not, not even in the false teeth of parental reproof, be wrong as to anything. The second circumstance is that he knows there has been reserved for him in heaven a very special place.

In short, he once had a mammy.

2

WITH a forlorn sense of impotence, one pauses here to reflect that, nowadays, in no household anywhere does one find an authentic mammy; so that whosoever speaks as to this vanished subdivision of fauna needs to depend upon a scant number of sexagenarians to divine exactly what he may be talking about. ——For the mammy, the true mammy, the mammy *au vieille roche*, is now extinct, along with the passenger pigeon and the bison and the hack driver; but in the Richmond of the 1880's a mammy still ruled over every household in which there were children.

So in no part of Richmond were mammies infrequent; but it was in Monroe Park that you noted them, upon clear afternoons, in full panoply. To every bench there would be two or three mammies; alongside most of the benches sprawled a baby carriage formed of rotund and elaborately betwisted wicker-work, of which the occupant was screened by a vividly blue veil; and whatever it was that mammies talked about, for some two hours, with a serene and oriental indolence, between their slow outbursts of sedate Olympian chuckles, you did not ever hear, because you were playing, in common with a select number of yet other children, under the uncompromising surveillance of all these mammies. Any one of them, at any instant, might direct toward you the attention of Sister Nelson with an acerb shrillness.

And besides that, when you played in Monroe Park, you had to be careful not ever, upon any imaginable pretext, to get your nice clean linen suit messed up; because, otherwise, you became just the most aggravating child that ever was.

3

THESE ladies wore white caps and large white aprons, befrilled proudly. They ran, rather, to stoutness; and to steel-rimmed spectacles they accorded a perceptible vogue. Each one of them was—legally, at any rate—a Negress. Each one of them some twenty years earlier had been a slave; but now they were tyrants. Not for one quarter-instant would I suggest that their despotism was often, or indeed ever, unkindly. I mean merely that none dared to assail the authority of the mammies of Richmond within the borders of their several kingdoms; and that this was especially true of the parents who paid to each one of them ten dollars a month.

I grant that in every household—in order, it is my theory, to cajole into self-complacence the cook and the house girl—the children's mammy was ranked, through a jocose flight of fancy, as being one of the servants. —For that, most precisely, is what a mammy was at no time whatever, except only upon the courteous principle by which a monarch elects, in state papers or in formal proclamations, to describe himself as being the servant of his people.

In brief, the mammy was a Virginian institution which, under the encroachments of democracy, has vanished; she survives only in the heart's core of her fosterlings; and she is not comprehensible any longer except by those who have need to remember her forever. The children of Virginia, so nearly as I can understand their unhappy estate, are looked after nowadays, more or less, by a visitant duchess, more or less Negroid, who stays with them for as long as the job contents her; and who passes on by-and-by to another nursery somewhere else. Her place is then filled, for a month or it may be for two months, by some other nomad; and later, by yet another. Thus Amurath to Amurath succeeds, barbarically. It must be, for these luckless children, rather like living in a world which every once in a while shoots off into space and finds an alien sun about which to revolve. It is, at any rate, a state of affairs which does not bear thinking about, by us who once had a mammy.

4

AND SO, while in theory I would like for a fair number of these children to be dealt with competently, by Mrs. Louisa Nelson, yet to the other side, Mrs. Nelson was my mammy; and she was by me regarded with an affection which, during some sixty years of research work, I have not found any other person to merit. Were she alive today, I with an incivic stoicism would observe every brat upon earth in transit toward a state reformatory rather than permit Mrs. Nelson to leave me. —For she was my mammy once, now, and forever afterward; so that I must decline, even in thought, to be severed from her by the dictates of altruism.

—Although, of course, she had not always been Mrs. Nelson. In fact, at the beginning, which was about 1820, she was just Louisa, when she belonged to Miss Patsy Brander. She was Miss Patsy's own colored girl; and every night she used to sleep in old Miss Patsy's room, in a trundle bed which enduring the day you stuck under Miss Patsy's big bed. That was so you could wait on Miss Patsy Brander, in case she wanted something, or if Miss Patsy got took sick in the night. She did, right often. And so Miss Patsy had a little stepladder to get in and out of bed with.

All this was sort of before Mammy had married up with Mr. Cornelius Winston, who belonged to

Miss Patsy too; and he was mighty handsome. He was always pleasant spoken. He toted fair with the high and the low. He was a fine good man. Mr. Winston was just the finest man that anybody ever knew. So he and Mammy were real happy together, in those bad old slavery times; and their daughter was named Kizzy. But Miss Patsy Brander up and died; and when her ownings got settled, Mr. Cornelius Winston was sold off to be the head butler for a white gentleman, that fancied him a heap, out West.

That was why Mammy did not ever see Mr. Winston again until after The War. He came back to her then, to find out how she and Kizzy were getting along; and he and Mr. Solomon Simms liked each other very much.

Mr. Solomon Simms was the other gentleman that Mammy was married to by this time. And Mr. Winston had married up too, to a colored lady in Kentucky; so he brought her picture along with him, and a picture of both the children, to let Mammy see what his family looked like. Mr. Winston was always mighty thoughtful. They were nice enough children; they took after Mr. Winston, you could tell that right off. The boy was his very living spit and image. But if you wanted an honest and true to God opinion, that fat, greasy-mouthed colored woman was kind of ornery-looking. Anyhow, Mr. Winston and Mr. Simms got along fine; and Mr. Winston stayed with them, out on the farm over in Powhatan County, for about two weeks.

After Mr. Winston went away, he sent back some presents for Kizzy, and along with them came a necklace of real coral beads for little Julia Simms, so as to keep her from having croup. Julia was Mammy's other daughter. You could always count on Mr. Winston to act handsome. And that was the last that Mammy ever heard about him. She most surely would have liked to find out what did become of Mr. Winston, when she had his street address out in Kentucky too, where he was setting up at catering and waiting on white people's parties; but then she and Mr. Winston never could get around to learning just how to read and write, what with all the other things they had to do.

And presently Mr. Simms, that nebulous and, as one somehow felt, that rather shiftless farmer— concerning whom, to the best of your recollection, you at no time heard anything quite definite, except only his delight in being honored with a visit by Mr. Winston, his all-gifted predecessor—Mr. Solomon Simms of Powhatan took sick and died. That was how Mammy came to marry Mr. Jeremiah Nelson, who was just as smart as you make them. He was right dark-complected, though.

Mr. Nelson was a city gentleman. He was born and brought up in Richmond. He had rooms upon

St. James Street. He worked for the *Richmond Evening State*. He packed papers.

One imagines, nowadays, this must mean that Mr. Jeremiah Nelson used to tie up, with very shaggy brown twine, and to deposit within the *State's* delivery wagons, those oblong bundles of printed matter which, later, at about five o'clock in the afternoon, when people were watering their front yards, and Mammy was wheeling John's baby carriage back home from Monroe Park, and you and Robert were walking alongside her, were flung out upon the red brick sidewalk, with an unforgettable massive slumping noise, and came pretty close to you sometimes, so that you held on to Mammy's skirts, while the enormous Percheron horse which drew the white-and-blue covered wagon continued its unhurried trotting toward wherever it was going.

One is not certain. One does not even know upon what principle those big bundles of newspapers were flung out upon the pavement, or who took charge of them afterward. One knows only that Mr. Nelson packed papers for the *Richmond Evening State* until the final 1870's, which was when Mr. Jeremiah Nelson died.

And to the very last, let it be observed, Mr. Nelson acted with more force of character than was displayed by Mr. Solomon Simms—who, so far as it can be remembered, did not even die of anything in particular. But Mr. Jeremiah Nelson died of pneumonia, just like that, and almost before you could snap your fingers, along about three days after he caught a bad cold in a snow storm; and it showed how careful you ought to be about not forgetting your rubbers.

That was why Mr. Nelson's widow kind of thought she might try working out, for a sort of change. She retained the rooms upon St. James Street. But she came to my parents when their first child was a month old, and when she was fifty-two, and she remained with us for the rest of her life.

5

It is a trait to be dwelt upon, the fact that after some threescore years of existence, Mrs. Nelson came to us when she was fifty-two, because never during the time that one knew her did her age vary. She was fifty-two. If pressed as to this point, through any ignoble considerations of arithmetic, or if reminded, with an unmannerly precision, as to the unusual number of years throughout which she had stayed fifty-two, she would so far yield as to concede that anyhow she was about fifty-two. Beyond that, there was no budging her, not even in her most lenient moments.

Now, technically, Mrs. Louisa Nelson was a Negress; but it is not conceivable that anybody ever said so in her presence, not even after she had become very deaf. She elected instead to rank as a colored person; and her color, to be precise, was the just not golden yellow of peanut butter. As to her parents it is not remembered that Mrs. Nelson ever spoke, but her features were unmistakably Indian; her eyes had the alert black gleam of undried ink; her nose hooked slightly; her lips were thin. She too was thin; and until she had passed eighty, a ramrod would have seemed, in comparison with Mrs. Nelson, to be liquescent. Upon her flat left breast, except only when she visited Monroe Park, or during yet more stately occasions which called for an appearance in her black silk dress, she wore two or three needles with thread in them; she had wholly beautiful white crinkly hair; and she smelled very pleasantly with an indefinable odor which I can but describe as that of musk flavored with cloth.

She must have had Negro blood, but in her exterior there was not any trace of it. She most certainly had a great deal of Caucasian blood; and one imagines that every drop of it was aristocratic. Mrs. Nelson, in any case, was.

She likewise was that patron saint who performed miracles for your comfort tirelessly; and who served as an efficient mediator between you and powers which (in academic theory) were stronger than Mrs. Nelson, such as unfamiliar policemen and God and large dogs and your parents. Parents were well enough in their place, and you loved both of them; but, relatively, their place was remote; and in it they now and then were engaged, with an irresponsible graveness, by grown-up affairs in which you were not interested.

Mrs. Nelson had no such frivolous avocations. To her children (a heading under which she did not include Julia and Kizzy, or any of Kizzy's descendants, but restricted to your two brothers and you) she devoted twenty-four hours of each day—excluding only her Sunday afternoons and her Thursday evenings out. She went then to her rooms upon St. James Street. She was Head of the Subobinate Department of the Tents of Ham and the Daughters of David; and upon St. James Street the members of this organization were accustomed to confer with Sister Nelson as to matters which she could not talk to you about, because they were Lodge secrets.

You did not mind the Sunday afternoons, when company came in or else you went out with your parents somewhere, and were allowed to be company yourself, and to let people see your raising, just as Mrs. Nelson had told you to do. But Thursday evenings were lonesome, after you had gone to bed, and the gas jet out in the hall had been turned down, and when both your brothers were asleep. Robert talked in his sleep a great deal, but that was not any help. As you remembered it afterward, there was always a soft-coal fire in the room upon those long Thursday evenings; and this made the shadow of the mantelpiece, upon the wall above it, jump every which way, like a big black chained-up Something, such as might be a Carpet-bagger, that was trying to get loose with no friendly intentions.

So you did not ever quite fall asleep until after Mrs. Nelson came in at twenty minutes after eleven. She said that you ought to have been asleep long ago. She asked if you children had been good children, and not kept everything in a swivet the first minute her back was turned. She brought you a glass of water, because you said you were sort of thirsty. That was so you could touch her. Then she got into her bed, which was next to your bed; and you went to sleep in less than no time, because everything was all right now that Mammy was back.

6

So LONG as Mrs. Nelson stayed near you, all matters tended to straighten themselves out satisfactorily. Even when you were sick-in-bed (for until you were at least ten years old you thought of this condition

as being one word) she saw to it that you were not
very sick, and had a plenty of boiled custard, and
in fact, rather enjoyed yourself. But she remained
rigid. She was not touched to the quick, nor did she
condole, when you were sick-in-bed. It was her official attitude upon all such occasions that you were
just upsetting the house from top to bottom by being
sick-in-bed. —For there was not anywhere one
minim of tenderness in Mrs. Nelson's nature, nor
any reasonableness either, but only an unlimited
devotion to her children.

So did it follow that at all times her ideas as to
corporal punishment stayed sound and unshakable.
To begin with, she did not ever concede that in any
circumstances any one of her children had been
bad; at utmost, the small accused might have been,
it was allowed fair-mindedly, sort of mischeevous,
but then, good Lord, what child would not be, when
folks started in to upset him like that without attend-
ing to their own business? Through this dashing
gambit, any parentally discussed punishment, instead of figuring as the result of a misdemeanor, was
left unmasked as the true cause of it.

The child had been mischeevous because folks
who were more than twice as big, and who did not
know how to keep their temper, had started in to
spank him, and what child, what child anywhere
upon this earth, would not be? That, and that alone,

was just simply what the indignant dark lawyer for the defence wanted to ask of Dr. Cabell and Miss Annie; and did ask, freezingly.

Moreover, should the incriminated parent remain deaf to remorse, then promptly the exposed rear of the condemned was shielded by both of Mrs. Nelson's lean and wiry, peanut-butter-colored hands. Nor from this strategic position was she detachable. So the foiled parent, or it might be both parents, withdrew. And Mrs. Nelson, triumphant but still icily offended, began to speak as to the convenience and the accessibility of her rooms upon St. James Street.

7

THROUGHOUT twenty-five years these rooms remained the weapon which made her always, at the last pinch, invincible. —For Mrs. Nelson did not have to stay where folks did not like her ways. She did not intend to go on slaving where people were not satisfied. And so, about once every month, we learned that she was going back home, the very first thing tomorrow morning, to live in her rooms over on St. James Street without being stormed at and fussed with enough to run anybody clean crazy.

I do not think that at any time she had the least intention of doing this. But the knowledge that she, after all, was free to desert us for those rooms upon St. James Street kept every one of her dependents in a proper state of subjection throughout the quarter of a century. —For Mrs. Nelson, of course, like all other authentic mammies, after her children had become too old to require a nurse, retained an anonymous ranking as a general assistant in our household affairs—and, at need, as their autocrat.

In title, to be sure, she remained Mammy. But so far as went her indoor pursuits, she merely swept, and dusted, and sewed, and excelled in darning, and delighted to wait at table in her black silk dress whensoever we had company. She tended the ill; she now and then cooked meals, but only when a creative urge to cook was upon her; and she "laundered" —if that verb be still in current usage—with a perfection which to the present age is unknown. In fine, Mrs. Nelson, after her actual retirement as a mammy, did everything; but always, it must be recorded, upon her own terms.

—Which reminds me to record likewise that Mrs. Nelson, what with all the other things she had to do, still did not ever quite get around to learning just how to read and write. So she remained unfamiliar with novels as to the South of yesterday, and she did not ever hear about any mammies who termed their children "my precious lamb," or "my own baby," or "honey chile," or yet something else of a nature no less affectionate and revolting. I am rather glad of this fact: for in Mrs. Nelson's eyes, these graceless if not actively immoral women would have ceased to figure as colored ladies; and in a brief philippic they would have been dismissed, I am wholly certain, as niggers who were just plumb idiots.

8

So THEN did the fourth part of a century pass by without forcing us to conceive of a life without Mrs. Nelson, or to face the notion of any existence thus maimed and bone-bare. Nor did we, until her death, when she was about eighty-five, had left us no choice; and for my part, it is a notion to which, after forty-and-some years of deliberation, I have not as yet become reconciled.

It should be recorded that upon the last day of her life, she told the attendant physician she was fifty-two; as well as that, upon this same heart-breaking Sunday, when she was not permitted to leave her bed, she assured me that, the very first moment she got over this sort of sinking spell, she meant to go straight spang back to her rooms, over on St. James Street, and not be a bother to us, when once she was out of this bed, praise the Lord.

—Because it was getting right far past the time for

her little biddy bed to be pushed back under Miss Patsy's big bed. That was why she was trying to get up, Mrs. Nelson explained. So please be good kind folks and let her get out of bed.

She, who had been indomitable, now spoke half timidly. She did not know any one of us. In her last thoughts we figured as unfamiliar, and it might be cruel, white persons who were interfering with the proper duties of Miss Patsy Brander's own colored girl, under the presidency of Andrew Jackson, now that Mrs. Nelson had put out of mind those twenty-five years of tyrannic devotion which she had given to us, "her children," and of which no mortal that ever lived could hope to be worthy. She had forgotten about Julia, and about Kizzy, and about her three husbands, even Mr. Cornelius Winston. With a child's fitful and half-hushed persistence, she repeated that Miss Patsy Brander wanted to have her room kept right enduring the day time; and it was in this way that Mrs. Nelson left us, in an attempt to wait upon her first mistress, who had been buried for somewhat more than sixty years.

9

ALMOST at random I have set down these recollections, as to an illiterate and hard-headed and great-hearted Negress, just as I thought about them, and without any re-arrangement or recoloring, because to my judgment Mrs. Nelson explains several generations of not humble-minded Virginians. Every one of these Virginians once had his mammy; by her he was taught, from infancy onward, to regard himself as an all-superior person; by her he was spoiled, completely and forever; and by her, as he very well foreknows, he by-and-by is going to be put in his right heavenly place, not unseverely, with an injunction, for the good Lord's sake, to behave himself now, and to let people see his raising.

In view of these circumstances, I submit, the aforesaid Virginian should not, in common reason, be required to affect any mock modesty. He is of the elect; he willy-nilly has been made a sophomore seraph; and for him to deny the fact would be a sacrilege.

—For do you but consider the plight of my own generation. It is wholly certain that all those mammies who once forgathered in Monroe Park are now assembled on an eternally clear afternoon somewhere in heaven. It is just such a partly Hebraic and partly Baptist heaven as they expected, because God, if that were necessary, will have rebuilded it especially so as to prevent their being disappointed. But they will not be seated upon thrones unsociably. Instead, there will have been provided an infinity of broad benches, with room upon every one of them for three persons inclining toward stoutness; these benches will be molded of bright gold, I imagine; and they will be decorated suitably with all the gems which St. John mentions.

Nor will any one of these dark angels wear a long white robe such as, to a respectable colored person, could not but indecorously suggest nightgear. They instead will all wear black silk dresses of the very best quality, as well as befrilled caps and large aprons, and extra-large, loose golden slippers. And everywhere about them, but always under their uncompromising surveillance, will be frolicking obediently a throng of deceased Virginian lawyers and bankers and physicians and tobacconists and clergymen and, I daresay, a few convicts. —For the fact has been explained to Jehovah, quite firmly, that while upon earth all these Virginians, at their very worst, were just sort of mischeevous.

So then do the mammies of the 1880's as yet talk lazily together forever and ever, between their slow benignant chuckles, while these blessed spirits await the complete return of their children. And eventually, some one or the other of them will be inquiring —without, I am afraid, any special enthusiasm,—

"Ain't that your Jeemes, Sis' Nelson?"

Everything will be all right then.

Part Nine 𝕰

"PUBLISHED IN RICHMOND, VIRGINIA"

The editors are retiring from the editorial field with this issue. We have made some people exceedingly angry and we have encountered blank indifference from an even larger number. We have also had an enormous amount of fun. If we had possessed either wisdom or experience we would not, quite carelessly, at a Sunday afternoon party, have launched a penniless magazine. We are happy beyond words that we lacked both wisdom and experience, for we would not have missed The Reviewer *for anything in the world.*

Editors of THE REVIEWER (*October, 1924*)

1

WHEN some as yet to be born historian prepares to deal candidly with that which Virginians of the first quarter of the twentieth century thought to be their civilization, then his will be the task to discover through what miracle, or art, or accident, four youngsters caused Richmond-in-Virginia to become a literary center between the February of 1921 and the October of 1924.

I, who witnessed the entire wonder-working, throughout and at close quarters, cannot aid him. I know merely that during these three years and eight months *The Reviewer*, as "owned and edited" by Emily Clark and Margaret Freeman and Mary Dallas Street and Hunter Stagg, did exist as an *ignis fatuus* without any fellow in our cultural dusk.

Emily Clark has set forth, in her *Innocence Abroad*, the story of *The Reviewer's* career so handsomely, and with such ingratiating malice, that her account must remain always, I think, a source-book for the student, not merely of Virginian culture, but of American letters at large during the flamboyant Age of Mencken. And it was of this strange era in general, but of *The Reviewer* in particular, that I fell to meditating a brief while ago, when chance laid upon me an obligation to write concerning the *Messer Marco Polo* of Donn Byrne—inasmuch as when *The Reviewer* had just begun, and when in its never ending imbroglios I served as diagnostician, it was Margaret Freeman who introduced me to this romance. She had not read it, but the Century people had sent it to *The Reviewer*, and a tiny little bit of a book by an author nobody ever heard of did not seem worth while for Hunter to be bothering about in a notice of it, or did I think so?

Standing, I read as chance prompted, upon page 90, where I found Li Po to be saying:

"Often times I do be feeling sad, and thinking of the friends of my youth who are gone. Yuan Chen, who might have been a better poet nor me, if he had been spared; and H'sieng and Li Chien, too. Ah, they were great poets, Golden Bells. They never sang a poor song, Golden Bells, that they might wear a fine coat. And they'd write what was true, wee mistress, were all the world to turn from them. And I'm the laureate now, the court singer, living in my glory, and they're dead, with their dreams. I'm the last of the seven minstrels. And, wee Golden Bells, I do be thinking long."

2

It was a prose passage which, as the illiterate say, "intrigued" me. I liked it, somehow, upon grounds I could not define, because it seemed a queer medley, thus to find a Chinese poet of the eighth century alive some five hundred years later and speaking in the dialect of John M. Synge, or rather in the true Kiltartanese of Lady Gregory; but I did not argue with Margaret Freeman (who, while I read, had waited with her chin raised defiantly), inasmuch as even in those primal days of my acquaintance with *The Reviewer,* I had learned that to argue with any-one of its proprietors, those voluble and ardent in-fants, was time-wasting. With a self-protective vagueness, I agreed "to see about it"; and I left 809½ Floyd Avenue, carrying along with me *Messer Marco Polo* to be weighed at less precarious leisure.

When I read the tiny book I liked it entirely, nor did I veil my enthusiasm. So did it happen that I re-viewed *Messer Marco Polo,* for *The Nation,* with a frank confessing that because of the delight which I had got from this romance, I almost certainly was writing a vast deal of high-pitched nonsense such as, later, I would be regarding with fidgets. And the publishers reprinted as much of this review as could be got upon the back of the book's dust wrapper, be-cause in those days I passed as a quite famous writer.

And I thus seemed to figure both as the small book's discoverer and as its chief patron throughout the next seven or eight years, during which *Messer Marco Polo* went into edition after edition, chaperoned by my approval; and during which the "first issue," even that same scorned copy which I had carried away from *The Reviewer's* offices in a side alley, attained a market price such as if I were to record it here would convict me of being a completely untrustworthy person.

3

OF *The Reviewer*, therefore, and of that flashing brief season of Virginian culture which it impelled, I fell to thinking when, at Poynton Lodge, I returned to the book I had read first at Dumbarton Grange. How long it had been since I looked into *Messer Marco Polo*, I did not remember, and for this reason I opened the tiny tan-colored volume with trepidation. —For to re-encounter, after well domesticated years of severance, one's former loves, in literature as in life, is an experience not always exhilarating. Only too often do they arouse a derisive wonder, along with embarrassment, and flushed, vagrant, morbid speculations as to your taste, or as to your sanity even, during those fled Aprils in which any such lumbering triteness could have seemed all-glorious.

If I began dubiously, yet by-and-by I read with increasing contentment. Here the old magic had not died. It was hardly dimmed. If somewhat I deplored an occasional saccharinity, the eye passed quickly over it, nor did the mind long retain it. And if somewhat—nowadays—I resented the infused Gaelic element where it did not appear to me essential, that was merely because of my too complete knowledge as to Donn Byrne's later career. In this special book his perpetual and maddening insistence upon the, after all, not wholly unique distinction of being an Irishman, had done him as an artist no grave hurt, not as yet. Later, it bludgeoned his fine talents blatantly.

Still, then, I found *Messer Marco Polo* to be a splendid and sumptuous romance, but I found it also a pathetic wee ghost. In common fairness, you observe, I cannot well talk about Donn Byrne without using that ubiquitous "wee" which infests even his most lordlike prose passages, somewhat as lice prey upon lions. —For to me this book spoke not merely of the dead glories of Venice in her heyday, or of the perished magnificence of the great Khan, Kubla, but of that faraway year of true grace, 1921, when *Messer Marco Polo*, in common with *The Reviewer*, was first published.

The book spoke, to me at least, of an incredibly remote time when, under the stimuli of a strange brief renaissance, American fiction, in Stephen Leacock's apt phrase, was riding off furiously in all directions. This *Messer Marco Polo*, I remembered, was only a single one of the very many vivid phenomena of an all-vivid and zestful period during which perturbing and most variously admirable new novels appeared, as though in spates, plenteously; and when current fiction was received—that was the odd part of it—with excitement.

"Nowadays," I reminded myself, "no living person appears able to read a new novel, when it is superimposed upon him by his book club, with more than a few pallid sentiments of approval, politely restrained. We feel that mere fiction, except in the form of a political statement or an international agreement, is not really important."

I did not know the reason of this changed attitude, of this lessened receptiveness. I knew only that in the America of 1921 a new book could find readers, and indeed a host of readers, who, whether in their praise or censure, were ardent about it. Well, and if, to the one side, this was an era in which an obsessed continent fulminated concerning *Main Street* and *Winesburg, Ohio*, and *This Side of Paradise*, and in which a lynching party awaited H. L. Mencken at all points south of Maryland, this same 1921, when *The*

Reviewer began, was likewise the period of *Linda Condon* and of *Peter Whiffle* and of *Autumn* and of *Jennifer Lorn* and of *The Hard-Boiled Virgin*, as well as of *Messer Marco Polo*. In brief, America noted, in that era of more ardent readers, an ensorcelled handful of bemused fiction writers who pursued, more or less profitably, an elaborated and burnished style.

4

"AND with results now how alien!" I reflected, as in the glowing saga of *Messer Marco Polo* I observed passage after passage each one of which was a self-evident and self-conscious exercise in begemmed writing.

"Here is no paragraph," I remarked, "but betrays an unwearied quest of loveliness and leans shamelessly toward refinement of diction. In this *Messer Marco Polo* hardly anywhere can one find a sentence which is not an unmodish small miracle; for the entire brief book is beautiful; and we have, nowadays, no living writer as yet indulging untimeworn flesh and blood who is capable of composing any half-page among these 147 pages."

Even so, I conceded that, to the best of my knowledge, no one of our more widely honored tale-tellers, during late years, had cherished the least desire to

write in this fashion, inasmuch as my young seniors
in literary seriousness appeared to have dismissed,
with unconcealed abhorrence, the notion that a
writer might advantageously know anything about
writing.

Then to myself I remarked also: "The cult of
elaborated prose is as far out of date as the corset, as
obsolete as the epigram, as quelled as a congress-
man. And it really does seem rather a pity to a misled
squad of now senescent persons who once looked
upon authorship as being a fine art."

5

DISMISSING these weighty reflections, I reverted con-
sideringly toward *Messer Marco Polo* and to yet another aspect which the book reveals nowadays. I
mean the uniqueness of this tiny romance, if not of
necessity in all earth's literature, yet its most certain
and surprising uniqueness among the long list of
books by Donn Byrne. —For not only was this his
best book: the point is that no one of his other romances has really anything in common with *Messer
Marco Polo*. The others are not ill done; they enter-
tain: and indeed, they maintain an exceedingly
high level of competence and of grace in writing.
But they lack, and they all lack utterly, the special,

the incommunicable, small, tender, valiant magic of *Messer Marco Polo*.

Truly, each writer who is at all remembered must become hazily thought about at wide intervals, in the large range of posterity's more vital interests, as the author of his supreme book alone. Yet, as the rule, he will leave behind him, to survive sparsely among his especial admirers, some number of books, or at least one book, of which the twinkling differs from the coruscations of his acknowledged master-work in degree rather than in kind. This, most precisely, is what Donn Byrne did not do. Instead, so nearly as I can phrase it, after unloosing, in his fourth book, an unlooked-for comet which swam into the ken of all literate star-gazers, he went back, for the rest of his life, to his momentarily put-by vending of a superior sort of verbal candy. And a heavenly body, even though it be only an asteroid, has not anything in common with bonbons. There is no known scale of comparison.

The disparity, I repeat, is unusual. In fact, I do not recall but one other author by whom a display of clear genius has been confined, thus wholly and thus sharply, to just one book. At first glance, Cervantes figures as a majestic analogue: but then *Don Quixote* is, after all, not one book but two books, produced separately, a decade apart. And Mrs. Calvin Ellis Stowe, it is true, wrote copiously in addition to *Uncle Tom's Cabin* nothing else whatever of which even the title can be recollected, nowadays, except through a deplorable wasting of research work; yet I question if many persons regard *Uncle Tom's Cabin* as an epos of other than antiquarian interest, or very often read it except under coercion.

As a parallel to Donn Byrne, I can think only of the Mrs. William Gaskell, of Manchester in England, who wrote *Cranford* as well as this and the other novel, every one of which has descended into oblivion's maw a large deal deeper than ever plummet sounded or any except the merely professorial pursued—leaving *Cranford* serenely immortal and always to be adored, upon its own sparingly ornamented, tiny, cool altar.

Elizabeth Cleghorn Gaskell, in a middle-Victorian Lancashire rectory, and Bryan Oswald Donn Byrne, of that no less obsolete Brooklyn which turkey-trotted, compose a droll-seeming conjunction. Yet the parallel, I think, exists. Among the haphazard company of those who, at one time or another, have written adroit and permanent and well colored English prose, it is with these two alone—to my finding—that genius has dwelt briefly but lovingly, in order to beget, as offspring of the divine liaison, perfection, before quitting them forever. You cannot but admire the sardonic apologue, if only because it has not any possible moral.

6

MEANWHILE I may appear to have strayed somewhat from the unparalleled three years and two-
thirds of a year during which Richmond-in-Virginia
figured as a literary center. It was in the November
of 1920 that, in this city, four young persons who
combined literary leanings with an aggregate bank
account of $200.75 decided to found a magazine;
and so the first issue of *The Reviewer* became pur-
chasable in the February of 1921, as "owned and
edited" by Emily Clark and Margaret Freeman and
Mary Dallas Street and Hunter Stagg. It was not
purchased, however, beyond the limits of decorum.
The Reviewer began as a semi-monthly magazine;
it then shifted to a monthly publication; in 1922 it
took shape as a quarterly; and toward the close of
1924 it was presented gratis to Paul Green, who at
this time was with the University of North Carolina,
at Chapel Hill, where *The Reviewer* outlasted yet
one more calendar year.

Now, in Richmond, *The Reviewer*, which started
with a capital of $200.75, did not ever materially in-
crease or diminish that capital; it carried virtually
no advertising to aid its income; and not any contributor received one penny for such of his or of her
writings as *The Reviewer* deemed to be worthy of its
pages. Haughtily, *The Reviewer* announced, upon

the inside of its front cover, that "the payment for such MSS. as may be found available will be in fame not specie."

And the egregious-seeming promise—here looms the miracle—was kept: for not merely did *The Reviewer* publish articles by almost every noted American writer of the period; from Europe likewise it drew upon glittering sources; and *The Reviewer* "discovered" not fewer than a dozen young American authors who were destined to become applauded, at least temporarily, and all whose first published writings were published in Richmond, Virginia, by *The Reviewer*.

For the benefit of that same unborn Virginian chronicler to whom I alluded at outset, let it here be recorded that among those who contributed to *The Reviewer* were: Achmed Abdullah, Hervey Allen, Hansell Baugh, Henry Bellaman, Edwin Björkman, Ernest Boyd, Barrett Clark, Aleister Crowley, Babette Deutsch, Charles Divine, Paul Eldridge, Ronald Firbank, John Galsworthy, Ellen Glasgow, Douglas Goldring, Paul Green, Sara Haardt, Joseph Hergesheimer, DuBose Heyward, Addison Hibbard, Robert Hillyer, Guy Holt, Gerald W. Johnson, Mary Johnston, Margery Lattimer, Amy Lowell, Arthur Machen, H. L. Mencken, Michael Monahan, Edwin Muir, Robert Nathan, Frances Newman, James Oppenheim, Hamilton

Owens, Julia Peterkin, Josephine Pinckney, Allen W. Porterfield, Burton Rascoe, Ben Ray Redman, Agnes Repplier, Cale Young Rice, Lynn Riggs, Amélie Rives, Lewis Piaget Shanks, C. Alphonso Smith, Lewis Worthington Smith, Vincent Starrett, Gertrude Stein, George Sterling, George Stevens, Allen Tate, Jean Starr Untermeyer, Louis Untermeyer, Carl Van Vechten, Henrie Waste, and Elinor Wylie.

The masterworks of these admired literati, and their ways, and their sayings, first and last, are they not written in the visions of Iddo the seer, or at any rate in the prophecy of Ahijah the Shilonite? It is a point as to which I am not wholly certain, literary fame being what it is in fragility.

Even so, I can assure you that, when *The Reviewer* reigned, every one of these aforementioned contributors did indeed glow with a resplendency more or less dazzling, or else they attained to some such incandescence a good while before the 1920's had ended, with America's forlorn bankruptcy as to almost all its artistic and political and monetary and moral tenets.

7

IN LITERARY columns and in editorials throughout the more or less United States of America, and in

Great Britain and her colonies likewise, *The Reviewer* during its short life was discussed as a harbinger and a portent of none knew just what. Freely, however, was *The Reviewer* reviewed "as the beginning of a great Southern literary renaissance." Authors, of all four sexes, both famous and nearly famous, came singly and in brisk shoals toward Richmond, on account of *The Reviewer*, that magazine without any exact peer, inasmuch as it was conducted for the diversion of its contributors; and to appear in *The Reviewer* became, throughout the insecure small world of American letters, a species of accolade.

Everywhere, in brief, except only in one of the United States of America, did English-speaking persons with literary tendencies appear to discuss with animation this unaccountable efflorescence of polite letters in Virginia. Virginia alone, it must be recorded, did not notice *The Reviewer's* existence. The magazine had few, or rather it had virtually no, subscribers in Virginia. It was glanced over, not without fretfulness, by an exceedingly scant number of Virginians. And Richmond, after having been made somehow a literary center, did not delight in the city's unfamiliar rôle.

The odd trouble was that the four young editors were more or less enfranchised as to our better drawing-rooms. Pretty much everybody, or at least everybody who, as we phrase it, "counted," knew Emily and Margaret and Mary and Hunter; they were accepted by the élite; and now that each one of them so often had literary guests "from out of town," you faced, unavoidably and continually, the question what to do about accepting these guests also?

8

SINCE all this happened so very long ago that one can plausibly declare our present-day Richmond to differ in every known respect from the Richmond of the 1920's, it may be allowable, for an antiquary, to record a few of the involved problems. One of these visiting authors, *The Reviewer's* mainstay, for example, was reputed to have published, somewhere, some articles—such as no well-bred person had ever considered reading—in which he spoke of the South as being backward as to literary culture; and to receive socially an irresponsible blasphemer of this stamp would be, it was felt, disrespectful to the memory of Father Ryan and of John Esten Cooke, as well as to Thomas Nelson Page, who was not merely an author but an ambassador, and had married into the largest department store in Chicago. Moreover, yet another one of those Northern writers who very often came to Richmond on account of

The Reviewer was, as somebody or other had told you only last Wednesday, a Jew.

I here face a point such as may not be dismissed by the irrelevant fact that the concerned author happened to be of Presbyterian Dutch origin; for in Richmond, at this remote period, if anybody, no longer ago than last Wednesday, had told you he was a Jew, then you at once became eager to admit the Jews were a wonderful people. The way they all stood together reminded the admiring Richmonder (during the faraway 1920's) of those brave little Japs when they licked the tar out of Russia.

It was merely that, in the homes of Richmond's pre-eminent Gentiles, one, just somehow, during the 1920's, did not encounter any professed Jew; nor into the festive gatherings of such luminaries did any Jew who had not become an Episcopalian enter. After office hours, the Jews of Richmond forgathered to dine or to dance or to marry, or more conclusively, to be buried, with one another. That these facts were an irrelated heaping up of sheer accidents all Richmond agreed. Richmond fostered no undemocratic social distinctions. Yet in view of these customary and so numerous accidents, just what, exactly, could anybody be asked to do about them?

A third author entered Richmond traveling, quite unchaperoned, with a young woman to whom, concededly, he was not married. He spoke of her, as if (in the face of any such brazen conduct) the assertion could at all matter, as being his literary agent. And no less far beyond reason was found to be the impenitence of yet another contributor to *The Reviewer*, who did not conceal—nay, but who flaunted, with an unsmiling impishness—the circumstance that, at his home in the North, he consorted with colored people as social equals: for here was a proceeding as to which Richmond (at this remote period) did not prattle, even editorially, about being broad-minded.

Nor did the visiting authoresses arrive unattended by detriments. As concerned one of them (who had written that perfectly awful book) a precedent of thirty-odd years' standing had been fixed, in 1888, by the case of Amélie Rives, after the publication of *The Quick or the Dead?* inasmuch as in the deep South the family of the younger writer ranked with the very best people, just as in Virginia did the Rives of Albemarle. So, when a daughter of either house had brought forth a volume touching upon matters about which no Southern gentlewoman was supposed to know anything, good breeding quietly led you, in public, to pretend not ever to have heard of the book which in private you discussed with abandon.

A second authoress, however—in addition to displaying a morbid concern with the modern status of Negroes, when there were so very many other much nicer things for Southern ladies to write about —came, it was undeniable, "from the wrong side" of her native state. —Which of course settled everything, including her. And the troubled matrimonial past of yet a third visiting woman writer so far offset, in the eyes of Richmond, her beauty and her genius as to make ineffective her fairly eminent parentage—which after all was but Northern.

In short, from the standpoint of Richmond's upper classes, there was almost always something just a little bit detrimental, socially, about these visiting "out of town guests" of Emily and Margaret and Mary and Hunter. It seemed wiser to ignore them and all their doings, very much as, some eighty-five years earlier, Richmond had ignored young Mr. Poe and his *Southern Literary Messenger*, politely, without any comment.

9

I RECORD these ancient provincialities because, to my judgment, they are far from being trivial. They explain not merely why *The Reviewer* was never cherished in Virginia. They indicate a number of matters which Virginia then thought, and had always thought, to be more important than were, as Mr. Ritchie expressed it, "the mere beauties of the

belles lettres." They show the conditions, or the
prevalent and the indefinable atmosphere rather,
in which from the first a Virginian-born writer
(prior to our present state of cosmopolitan broad-
mindedness, one need hardly add) was forced to develop his talents as he best might; and they account
somewhat, I submit, for the restrained results.

And I find too that matters which during the heyday of *The Reviewer* I inclined to resent begin to
put on, under time's handling, a mellow and an
ameliorating patina, as it were, of the admirable.
—For back of each objection to *"The Reviewer*
group" lay the supreme virtue of Virginia—which
I take to be loyalty toward one's own.

"We have"—said, in effect, the Virginia of the
1920's—"our own standards of morals and of racial
purity and of social degrees. We intend to keep faith
with these standards, not because we know them to
be faultless, but because they are ours. We have likewise our own writers; and that they are not perfect,
we may admit tentatively, inasmuch as we never
went so far as to read their books; even so, these
writers are ours: and we do not care to have them
dispraised by outsiders."

—All which was, of course, both provincial and
pig-headed. So I cannot say that I admire these dicta
as logic; but I do feel, nowadays, an heroic quality
in the sentiments prompting them. I incline, in

brief, under time's handling, to imagine that loyalty to one's own faith and kindred may, after all, be a more important matter than are "the mere beauties of the *belles lettres.*"

10

I NOTE that a leading virtuoso of these mere beauties has recorded for the benefit of posterity:

"Though it lived but briefly, *The Reviewer* marked a clean-cut phase in our literary history. . . . *The Reviewer* came upon the scene partly to stir up the South (it was the exact moment of Mencken's challenging 'The Sahara of the Bozart') and partly to carry forward the new sophistication of the literary group which then was the most influential in America. It was the day of Hergesheimer and Frances Newman and Mencken, and the eve of Elinor Wylie, Carl Van Vechten and the newly arrived Ellen Glasgow; these are among the people who fostered and wrote for *The Reviewer.* . . . Their attitude toward life—emphatically skeptical, ironic, cultivated, aristocratic—banished a gross romanticism and inaugurated writing of suavity and elegance.

"The era of sentimentality was now over; an adult outlook was gestating. Mr. Hergesheimer was remarking that to give large sums of money to the starving children of Europe 'was one of the least engaging ways in which money could be spent. *The Reviewer* was far more appealing.' Miss Clark was expressing the credo of her magazine: 'We cared little what our contributors said, if they said it well.' Carl Van Vechten was writing that he considered *Jennifer Lorn* 'one of the masterpieces of all time.' In such a soil *The Reviewer* flowered and briefly prospered. . . .

"The era of *The Reviewer* was a snobbish era, in which . . . facile suavity and elegance . . . led their admirers to believe that a patrician and mellow way of living and attitude toward life had reached the American scene. But those years were merely a false dawn, for this 'cultivation' was self-satisfied and negative, a drawing away from the real roots of American life, and hence useless as a civilizing factor. 'We cared little what our contributors said, if they said it well.' That is an epitome and a grave indictment."

11

—ALL which tends, more or less clearly, to show you the disastrous results that may follow when an outlook, howsoever adult, begins to gestate; as well as the extreme reprehensibility of publishing thirty-one small magazines for the contributors' amusement. You, my discerning reader, may object—after consulting the list of once famous authors which I have set down a bit earlier—that a fair number of persons who "fostered and wrote for *The Reviewer*" (which really does sound like a most serious offence) did not display in their writing any special tincture of an "attitude toward life" which was "skeptical, ironic, cultivated, and aristocratic." But I, being more tactful, grant humbly that no sound moralist ought to be bothered by inconsistent facts.

I plead merely that "*The Reviewer* group" (to which I had the honor to belong) did not comprehend how insidiously our small dinner parties were drawing away from the real roots of American life; nor could we foreknow that a roomful of friendly persons who had met to discuss each of one another's recent books and a moderate number of cocktails, concocted of Prohibitional liquors, were becoming (in such a soil) forever useless, if not indeed viciously detrimental, as a civilizing factor for "the American scene." We did not even notice that in the immediate neighborhood an outlook was gestating. We knew only that we found *The Reviewer* to be an amusing plaything.

12

As TO that so very far-off era of the 'twenties, when, at any rate occasionally, prose was gemmed and our

upper classes were gentry, I know likewise that authors then enjoyed writing their books; and that, as
I have said, these books evoked from their readers
a more lively response than any current book in-
cites nowadays. That the books of *The Reviewer's*
period did not have any large part in shaping our
civilization as it today exists, remains possible;
charity may at least hope so; and that few or none
of the books of the 1920's will be treasured up forever
as American classics, so as to become the compulsory
reading-matter of restive high-school students, appears conceivable.

The point, though, is that we of *"The Reviewer
group"* wrote for the pleasure of it; and we got this
pleasure. We heathen in our blindness did not grant
that moral earnestness, or even the most elevated
sort of patriotism, ought to be accepted as a substitute
for talent. We did not believe it was the main duty
of an essay writer or of a novelist or of a poet to
reform his land, or mankind in general, or even (I
am afraid) himself; and if, "as the small civilized
minority," we did assume—just tacitly, as a mere
matter of course—our own eternal fame in letters,
yet tacitly we did not think it at all important.

Far too utterly far gone were we in that which we
dubbed "sophistication." So one did not, we im-
agined, receive professorial theses as to the slight
demerits and the unique excellence of one's writ-

ing, nor were clipping bureaus patronized, beyond the tomb; and neither in paradise nor in any other more ardent eternal home was *The American Mercury*, as edited by H. L. Mencken on sale upon the fifteenth of every month, to function as the interred's arbiter in literary affairs. We wrote instead for the pleasure which we got out of writing—and out of being talked about, momentarily.

13

IT WAS an era, not of mere snobbishness, I submit, but of gusto, among both the writers and the readers of current books. And today, when the reasonably respectable reading-matter diffused by book clubs is accepted with the same resignation which we accord to the weather, there is no such gusto in our current letters, nor anywhere else in a tormented world which tends, quite naturally, to dislike and to blackguard all eras that were more fortunate.

Yet for one, I like to look back, with an Horatian melancholy, athwart the fugacious years, toward the conferences and the cocktail parties and the loquacious midnights when, Mencken being consul, *The Reviewer* was published in Richmond, Virginia. I think of those who are dead; I think of those who, with serene wisdom, put aside writing when writing had ceased to divert them; and I think, too, of yet others from the disbanded "*Reviewer* group" who, with not less wisdom, have continued to publish because writing still diverts them.

Their books are received politely; and their books for a brief period sell well enough; and yet, no sooner is each book published than the reading public unites, as it were, in a decorous funeral cortège to honor and to extol, but above all to get rid of, the object of their praise. —For these writers belong, irretrievably, to another era, to an alien, more carefree world, which has vanished; so their merits, even in the same instant that they are acknowledged, or commended, are dismissed as irrelevant; and *The Reviewer* seems as far away as *The Yellow Book*, or *The Rambler*, or *The Spectator*.

14

THUS then, in very much the necrologic vein of gaunt Villon, did I reflect concerning the zestful and fervent writers of the 'twenties, as they were in the gay prime of their fame and vigor, now that I put aside *Messer Marco Polo*, that pre-eminently "dated" book which had set me to thinking about 1921, when both it and *The Reviewer* came into being; and when so many of these writers were my intimates. But I first read, yet again, in this out-of-date, small tan-colored volume:

"Often times I do be feeling sad, and thinking of the friends of my youth who are gone. Yuan Chen . . . and H'sieng and Li Chien, too. Ah, they were great poets, Golden Bells. They never sang a poor song, Golden Bells, that they might wear a fine coat. And they'd write what was true, wee mistress, were all the world to turn from them. . . . And they're dead with their dreams. . . ."

It is a prose passage which does not any longer puzzle me.

Part Ten ৪৯

MISS GLASGOW OF VIRGINIA

I feel that the war has killed so much more than armies and human beings, that it has, in a way, put all artistic impulses into a long sleep, or into a trance of futility. But I wish we could have again, on this perfect summer afternoon, one of our old talks on writing and the kind of writing that was worth while. Even if we did not agree, our talk would be with the old friendship and sympathy.

ELLEN GLASGOW (22 *August 1945*)

ONE

1

Now that Ellen Glasgow is dead, I need to quote from the first article which I typed concerning the remarkable Commonwealth of Virginia, as far back as in the spring of 1925; and which began roundabout by remarking, in the *Nation,* that of all the novels published by Ellen Glasgow, prior to and including 1925, *Barren Ground* was, to my finding, her masterpiece. —For I still think *Barren Ground* to have been the most important of my dead friend's novels.

I record this statement (so did I continue in 1925) after a lengthy appraisal of the book's many forerunners. And in considering this list, I am surprised by two phenomena. One of them is the startling approach to completeness, presented by these books as a whole, of Ellen Glasgow's portrayal of social and economic Virginia since the War Between the States. The other is the startling announcement, upon the dust wrapper of *Barren Ground,* that "with *Barren Ground* realism at last crosses the Potomac."

Nobody disputes that upon dust wrappers wild statements appear to be as frequent as cardinal virtues in a cemetery. Yet this particular statement, when it is advanced, or at any rate countenanced, by the firm which now for some twenty-five years has been issuing Ellen Glasgow's novels, arouses a troubling suspicion that her publishers may have been regarding her books, all the while, as being pleasant, slight tales of the only sort which, prior to the appearance of *Barren Ground* (still to quote from this dust wrapper), had yet been written about the State of Virginia—"as a land of colonels, of old mansions, and of delicate romance."

Eventually, however (as a great Virginian has remarked), all authors must learn, through time's teaching and a large deal of vexation, how neatly the pranks of most publishers may be compared with the peace of God, as being equidistantly beyond understanding. I dismiss the enigma, with tact, tacitly. And no matter what her publishers may assert, I reflect, here in these books by Ellen Glasgow is an almost wholly realistic and but very slightly expurgated depicting of our present-day Virginia, along with some seventy-five years of Virginia's past. Here is a vast panorama of—upon the whole—six decades of well-mannered futility.

The land of Ellen Glasgow's birth and nurture, the land which in its senescence she has commemorated, has become, to her interpreting, an unmistakably barren ground, no matter how pleasantly it may be diversified, in some places, by scattered relics of yesterday—"the colonels and the old mansions"—and, in yet other places, by a vaticinatory rose-coloring of Virginia's immediate future such as none save extreme pessimists, I trust, would disparage as being "delicate romance."

So far as go the colonels and the old mansions, it seems plain that for the deciduous aristocracy of that commonwealth which most often and most resonantly figures in oratory as a mother and as a cornerstone and as a guiding star and as a cradle, Ellen Glasgow, in the double-edged phrase, has not any use—except only as bijouterie. The virtues, the high-bred vices and the graces of the unhorsed Virginian Cavalier have survived, not without pathos, their heyday; and they serve her turn. So, because of their ornamental qualities, she cherishes and she at need extols these matters, with the perturbing and cool amiability of a past mistress in the art of parenthetic malice. And the one element of approved romance to be found in Ellen Glasgow's books about our latter-day life in Virginia is so far from being outmoded that it remains always, after a fashion which I hope to indicate, quite actually the *dernier cri*.

2

IN *Barren Ground* we have a renewed but a more obvious hint as to what I take to have been its writer's philosophy, throughout very many books, in regard to the better-thought-of constituents of romance. This novel is the story of Dorinda Oakley, born in Virginia of the tenant farmer class, and getting, somehow, through an existence in which the traditionary ardors and anguishes of human life do not ever ascend to their advertised poignancy.

Love comes to you, in the form of Jason Greylock; and for the while love is well enough; but to the other side—when that also happens—being cast by this latter-day Jason for the rôle of a deserted Medea (not long after an unlegalized childish souvenir of the faithless lover is en route) proves to be not intolerable. You marry somebody else, because you like this middle-aged Nathan Pedlar well enough; and when your husband dies in due season, it makes an astonishingly slight difference.

Yet other lovers come, and pass out of your living, and some of them are well enough, but no one of them matters deeply. You preserve from the almshouse your first collaborator in amour, that Jason Greylock who once technically "ruined" you; he dies by-and-by as a dependent on your charity; and you are not conscious either of complacency or of sorrow, not exactly. You feel instead, with a sort of incurious resignation, that by and large the affair has turned out well enough.

No one of these romantic incidents, you find to-

ward fifty, has mattered at all lastingly. And when
Dorinda Pedlar, a woman who has succeeded in life,
a widely wooed but a convinced and contented
widow, and an ever-busy and prosperous land-
holder now in her own right, stands beside her first
lover's grave, one encounters this passage:

"Out of the whirling chaos in her mind, Jason's
face emerged like the face of a marionette. Then
dissolving as quickly as it had formed, it re-appeared
as the face of Nathan, and vanished again to assume
the features of Richard Burch, of Bob Ellgood, and
of every man she had ever known closely or remotely
in her life. They meant nothing. They had no significance, these dissolving faces; yet as thick and fast
as dead leaves, they whirled and danced there, dis-
appearing and re-assembling in the vacancy of her
thoughts."

3

Now these reflections, the exact may declare, are
here presented by Ellen Glasglow, not as a philosophy, but as Dorinda Pedlar's perhaps transitory state
of mind. Nevertheless, you will find that a great
many of Ellen Glasgow's protagonists attain to very
much this same state of mind before reaching the
end of the particular novel of Virginian life in which
each one of them figures. The experiences which,

by every known rule of romantic Southern tradition, ought to have mattered most poignantly have, in reality, "meant nothing."

—Not that Ellen Glasgow, any more than does life, permits her Virginians to remain in this state of mind. It is to this fact I have been approaching; and it is upon this point I would dwell, after having found an inspection of her final paragraphs, in her several novels prior to 1925, to be rather strikingly revelatory.

Thus, in *Life and Gabriella,* the much battered Mrs. Fowler is last seen as departing, high-heartedly, with her most recently acquired lover, "toward the future." By both departants the halcyon-like qualities of the future are taken for granted. At the end of *The Builders,* deserted Caroline Meade has been uplifted mentally through noticing that, "beyond the meadows and the river, light was shining upon the far horizon." And indeed a fair number of Ellen Glasgow's characters, toward the end of their printed histories, get spiritual comfort out of observing a light in the sky or in somebody's eyes.

In the last paragraph of *The Descendant,* Maria Fletcher is coming toward Christopher Blake "across the sunbeams" of an allegorically fine morning. *Virginia,* just when all seems darkest, and immediately after a wave of despair, like a mortal sickness, has swept over Mrs. Oliver Treadwell, ends with the cheering telegram, correctly punctuated by the Western Union and found upon a hitherto unnoticed table, "Dearest mother, I am coming home to you, HARRY." And in *The Miller of Old Church*, the newly made widower, staunch Abel Revercomb, becomes so far consoled when Molly Merryweather draws him with the light of her face, and with the quivering breath between her parted lips, that, because of this vision of all her womanhood in surrender, he can now find happiness well within his grasp.

Thus, time upon time, does Ellen Glasgow, after having evinced no parsimony in supplying her Virginians with trials and defeats and irrevocable losses, yet almost always manage to end, somehow, upon this brave note of recording her people's renovated belief in a future during which everything will turn out quite splendidly. It is the exact note of what I alluded to, a while earlier, as the last and indeed the expiring cry of romance.

4

JUST so does the Dorinda Pedlar of *Barren Ground*, some five or six pages after the momentarily depressing reflections which for your benefit I have set down in full, reflect yet furthermore that inasmuch as the rural scenery of Virginia is variable and quite frequently picturesque (here to abridge a somewhat luxuriantly poetic-prose passage), "the understanding soul can never remain desolate." She decides for this reason that the best of her life is still to come; and the book leaves her in a placid state of anticipation.

—For Ellen Glasgow comprehends the bi-pedal fauna of her chosen hunting ground far too well to boggle over the event that almost all mortal beings, toward fifty, do glimpse the truth as to their personal experience with romance—or to omit the more significant fact that, after having done so, they, with extreme haste and good sense, resort to narcotics in the form of fine fairy stories concerning tomorrow. Ellen Glasgow knows that after all imaginable trials and defeats and losses, life does, illogically and relentlessly, yet again fill up the battered human machine with fresh optimism, very much as when, at more palpable filling stations, fresh gasoline is pumped into an automobile; and the machine is thus kept going.

TWO

1

To THE effect which has been recorded I discoursed as to the State of Virginia and Ellen Glasgow in 1925.

Then later, in 1930, when the glittering and noisy and perhaps futile, but wholly soul-stirring "literary movement" of the 1920's—the opulent brisk Age of Mencken—had ended, with a commendable exactitude, in 1929, and with the famousness of few of its survivors unmaimed, I wrote again, in the *Books* section of the *New York Herald Tribune*, concerning our Virginian civilization as it had been interpreted by Ellen Glasgow. A definitive collection of her novels had just then begun to appear.

And the event (I remarked) is fortunate. It is praiseworthy, if but as indicating a vague elementary justice to exist, upon rather widely scattered occasions, even in literary affairs.

—For (I continued) the belatedness of Ellen Glasgow's general recognition as the foremost woman novelist thus far produced by the United States of America seems nowadays to have been extraordinary. She had been publishing for some twenty-eight years with a considerable, if varying, meed of popular success. Her vogue, even as a Southern writer, was distinctively third-rate, with Miss Mary Johnston and Mr. Henry Sydnor Harrison well in the lead. In fact, throughout these twenty-eight years Ellen Glasgow had published, as it were, in the obscuring shadow of the famousness and the large sales of Mary Johnston. Ellen Glasgow was that other Virginian woman who wrote books; and some of her books, in their season, had been fairly successful as merchandise.

Thus matters stood until the appearance of her fifteenth novel, when the 'twenties were well under way. *Barren Ground* was brought out in the spring of 1925. Then alone did it occur to anyone of any least importance, so far as I know, to appraise seriously the work of Ellen Glasgow by any æsthetic canons.

—For *Barren Ground* was unmistakably the work of an actual and a highly competent artist. Its sales, they tell me, were not enormous; but it got for Ellen Glasgow that intelligent sort of consideration which she had earned long ago, without ever receiving. It introduced her, in fine, to what I have seen described as the intelligentsia; and an appreciative audience thus found in her earlier books also those virtues and the craftsmanship which Ellen Glasgow had cultivated for twenty-eight years without critical detection. Meanwhile she was publishing *The Romantic Comedians* and *They Stooped to Folly,* with an accompaniment of ever increasing plaudits, now that the proper superlatives to apply to her were known by all the better-class reviewers.

The belatedness of this recognition, I repeat, seems extraordinary. Yet I think, too, there is to be found in the earlier work of Ellen Glasgow the influence of certain modes, then current, each one of which made directly for the timely and popular appeal of the book at the date of its publication, and each of which, as literary fashions shifted, had tended to hide the book's merit as a work of art.

Those early books were very, very, and yet again very, generously proportioned: the general book-buying public is always favorably impressed by a visibly long book, if but upon the thrifty principle of getting your money's worth. When these books were written the ghost of Thomas Nelson Page still haunted everybody's conception of the South, keening in Negro dialect over the Confederacy's fallen glories; yet another Sentimental Tommy had made familiar the dialect of Thrums; and a number of persons were reading the Wessex novels of Thomas Hardy with an admiration which appears inexplicable. In brief, these earlier stories about the State of Virginia were written at a time when novels in dialect were prevailingly popular. Moreover, these books were written at a time when all American novels ended happily, as a polite matter of course.

These things are trivial. These things are, in every case, extraneous to the main matter of the book wherein they occur. Yet it was just these things, I believe, which for so long a season had combined to make many of those earlier books by Ellen Glasgow appear, to the casual eye, somewhat stolid- and wholesome-looking, a good while after stolidity and wholesomeness had been expunged from the list of possible literary virtues.

Today we declare that Ellen Glasgow was never stolid, and that "wholesome" is precisely the last adjective which any patriotic Southron would ever hurl at her. Today we recognize that in these superficial matters Ellen Glasgow conformed to the mode of her day very much as she then wore her beautiful bronze hair à la Pompadour. My point is merely that it was this wise-seeming conformity, I think, which delayed the recognition of Ellen Glasgow's importance.

2

—For, as I have pointed out in another place, you have in the work of Ellen Glasgow something very like a complete social chronicle of the Piedmont section of the State of Virginia since the War Between the States, as this chronicle has been put together by a witty and observant woman, a poet in grain, who was not at any moment in her writing quite devoid of malice, nor of an all-understanding lyric tenderness either; and who was not ever, through any tiniest half-moment, deficient in craftsmanship. You have likewise that which, to my first finding, seemed a complete natural history of the Virginian gentlewoman throughout the last half-century, with all the attendant features of her lair and of her general habitat most accurately rendered. But reflection shows the matter to be a great deal more pregnant than I thought at outset; for the main theme of Ellen Glasgow, the theme which in her writing figures always, if not exactly as a Frankenstein's monster, at least as a sort of ideational King Charles's head, I now take to be The Tragedy of Everywoman, As It Was Lately Enacted in the Commonwealth of Virginia.

3

You will note that almost always, after finishing any book by Ellen Glasgow, what remains in memory is the depiction of one or another woman whose life was controlled and trammeled and distorted, if not actually wrecked, by the amenities and the higher ideals of our Virginian civilization. The odd part of this is that it so often seems a result which the authoress did not foreplan, and more often than otherwise, an outcome which by no system of logic follows, of necessity, from the "story" of the book. It is merely that, from the first, Ellen Glasgow has depicted all gentlewomen—and in some sort, every one of her feminine characters—as being the victims of Virginia's not utterly unadvertised Southern chivalry. That is a conviction to which the faith of Ellen Glasgow has been given with a whole-heartedness such as no other belief has ever awakened in her nature; and it follows that whensoever she touches upon this conviction, her fervor ignites.

I turn, for example, to the earliest written of the books which Ellen Glasgow has chosen to preserve in her collected works. When the story of *The Battle-Ground* is gone by, what I recall most clearly are the contented bustlings about of Bettie Ambler and of Mrs. Lightfoot after having been rescued from the pampered estate of well-to-do Virginian gentlewomen by the grossness of war. These ladies, as you may remember, when once they had been released from their sheltered exaltation, got a sort of picnicking delight out of the uncivil realities by which men were appalled.

"But then the Major," as Mrs. Lightfoot observed, forgivingly, about her husband, "is a romantic at heart, and he is still surprised when human nature acts like human nature."

Thus clearly did Ellen Glasgow state her main complaint against the well-born male Virginian, as far back as in 1902. She has repeated it, since then, with accents which have lessened steadily in condonation.

4

WHAT remains in memory after *The Deliverance* has been finished, is that incisively symbolic figure of Mrs. Blake, blind and forever imprisoned in an ancient chair—an heirloom, of course,—and kept drugged with chivalrous lies. *Virginia* is, throughout, a summing up of the deficiencies, as a social unit, of that shielded and stainless gentlewoman who remains indigenous, even nowadays, to the postprandial adulation of politically ambitious Virginians. This story of Virginia Pendleton is, in short, a tragicomedy of the woman who conforms in all respects to her native state's notions of perfection. And lastly, *They Stooped to Folly* is the tragi-comedy of three women who conform, variously, to the desires of a Virginian gentleman as a mammal rather than to the demands of his caste.

My point is that, to Ellen Glasgow's finding, the conformist and the non-conformist to the Virginian's chivalrous ideas about women are punished with an equal sureness. Where the one is drowned in reprobation, the other is stifled in mind and spirit, with chivalry serving in either case as the executioner.

I regret to pursue, or even to mention, a notion so deplorable. Yet I think of Angelica Blackburn, in *The Builders*, inane and ruthless and secure upon that pedestal to which our Virginian chivalry has lifted the Virginian lady; of her elder and very near kinswoman, Angela Gay (in *The Miller of Old Church*), who had surrendered all activities and obligations in order to obtain the privileges of an invalid gentlewoman, from whom must be hidden away any unpleasant happening; and of Angela's sullen spinster sister, also, whose career as an artist had been denied to her by the circumstance that "it was out of the question for a Virginia lady to go off by herself and paint perfectly nude people in a foreign city."

I think of that fine desiccating flower of Virginian womanhood, Amanda Lightfoot, in *The Romantic Comedians*—who herself had not ever any need to think about anything, because all problems had been decided for her "by the appropriate feelings of a lady and the Episcopal Church." I think of Gabriella Carr, in *Life and Gabriella,* who, after the hard years had taught her some little wisdom, ran away, in a panic, from the most faithful and the most chivalrous of Virginian gentlemen because she could not endure being married to his delusions.

I think of all these luckless women, I repeat, and of yet other women whose histories have been recounted by Ellen Glasgow. And everywhere I find the problem: What is a woman to do before the top-lofty notions which are entertained by the romantic Virginian male as concerns women? Is it best to conform to these notions, at the cost of a cankering dishonestness and of a futile pottering over ever-present small household tasks? or to ignore these notions, at the cost of a chilled and futile spinsterhood not over-patiently endured by the casual charity of your nearer and less sympathetic relatives? or to rebel against these notions by letting "human nature behave like human nature," at the cost of acute discomfort and of ostracism and, in the end, of futility?

Such is the problem which in its every solution involves futility. Such is the problem which Ellen Glasgow tacitly declares to have been, in the Commonwealth of Virginia, throughout the last fifty-odd years, The Tragedy of Everywoman—for all that Ellen Glasgow has found it a tragedy of the mixed Jacobean school, in which the comic scenes are as plentiful as the sad ones; and it is the former which she touches up with the larger gusto.

5

I SHALL not further pursue this theme, because it is an embarrassing theme. Ellen Glasgow and I are the contemporaneous products of as nearly the same environment as was ever accorded to any two writers. From out of our impressions as to precisely the same Richmond-in-Virginia, she has builded her Queensborough, and I my Lichfield; yet no towns have civic regulations more widely various. Within but a few city blocks of each other, she waited a sad long time, as I, for comprehension to ring the doorbell. Waiting, she wrote her salty reams about chivalry, in the while that within a stone's throw, I was sprinkling upon the same topic sugar.

Yes: the coincidence, as well as the contrast, appears odd. And I find the outcome of it all, in the shape of our finished books, to be troubling. The outcome allows to me no hope that this over-logical woman does not consider me too to be "a romantic at heart"—and must thus dismiss all my toplofty and age-old notions serenely. The outcome would seem even to suggest that the one or the other of us may be wrong.

Yet I prefer to interpret it as proving only that never while life lasts can the two sexes quite understand each other. This is perhaps a rule which holds always and everywhere. Ellen Glasgow and I have attested that it very rigidly holds in Virginia.

Moreover, I observe that when, after some twenty-eight years of writing within the limits which befitted a Virginian gentlewoman (with disquieting overtones), Ellen Glasgow departed from this seemingly discreet course by publishing, in *Barren Ground,* an at least relatively unladylike book, she forthwith attained for the first time an appreciative and appreciable audience—although not in Vir-

ginia, of course, until after she had been properly
endorsed in New York and Boston and Chicago. I observe that when she more or less emulated the not
unfamous old monk of Siberia, at the high cost of
deriding the higher moral tenets of Virginia, in *The
Romantic Comedians,* and yet again in *They Stooped
to Folly,* then Ellen Glasgow became a major figure
in her publishers' lists. As a loyal Virginian, I deduce
with regret that the wages of sin may turn out to be
art of a remunerative quality.

THREE

1

To THE same critic of Virginian civilization, but from
a different angle of approach, I returned, after an
even dozen of her collected and revised novels had
been brought forth as "A Social History of Virginia,
from the decade before the Confederacy," by remarking that, when I considered Ellen Glasgow as
a person, she aroused in me a dark suspicion.

—For I fear (I continued, in a privately issued
pamphlet, of which, to be precise, exactly 109 copies
were issued in 1938) that she is a gentlewoman as
well as a genius in an era unfavorable to either ca-
pacity. I am certain that even if she had not ever

completed that mordant chronicle of Virginian
mores which blind fortune has lately bestowed upon
an unmeriting world, in a guise suitably handsome,
she would yet remain none the less a personage.

A little too much has been made, I think, of Ellen
Glasgow's revolt against the lofty traditions of the
Old South. Beyond any question, as a writer, she has
viewed these traditions with polite disrespect. Yet,
as a person, she very sensibly has fallen in with that
formalized and amiably luxurious manner of living
to which, virtually, she was born, not violating that
manner but simply making it more ample, and
modernizing it, in that dignified, middle-Victorian
mansion which, ever since Ellen Glasgow began to
be reviewed with woodcuts, has figured as the "town
house" of a long line of Glasgovian ancestors. She has
remained, in brief, as a person, somewhat the *grande
dame;* and as one result of this, she is not lightly
approachable. In her presence you treat your P's
and your Q's with all proper respect.

Otherwise, you are banished. I myself have been
exiled from court, any number of times, because of
an irreverence which approached lèse majesté, and
have had to ignore such mandates.

I forget just how many persons live in Richmond;
but I do know that several hundreds of them
nurture the as yet foiled ambition of being "invited
to Miss Glasgow's." Well, and they never will be "in-

vited to Miss Glasgow's," because of this or the other
delinquency, whether in charm or in intelligence
or in what we Virginians still refer to, in our quaint
way, as "breeding." This leads to despair and heart-
burning, and occasionally to yet other results.

For example, a good two years ago, when Ellen
Glasgow was entertaining in honor of Gertrude
Stein, upon a scale suitably splendid, an admirer of
Miss Stein made bold to attend the reception without
being invited. What happened then is still talked
about in Richmond; and I am sorry I cannot relate
in this place just what did happen. What happened
was peculiarly tragic, and indeed demolishing, from
the offender's point of view; and I can assure you the
offence will not ever be repeated.

Ellen Glasgow, then, as a person, is candidly exclusive. If you take that to imply any snobbishness,
you are wrong beyond the limits of my vocabulary:
I do not know of any living creature more magnanimous, except as concerns a not wholly flattering
press notice, or more affable than is Ellen Glasgow. It is simply that she does not cherish the dull
or the tacky; and being under no compulsion to put
up with them, doesn't. To the large host of her
personal friends, there is no woman more trust-
worthy, more exhilarating, more generous, more
complaisant, or more dear; and in fact a dangerously
great number of these friends make a sort of cult of

her. If they have not spoiled Ellen Glasgow during all these years, that is merely because she was born unspoilable. Nobody, of course, ever, quite, is.

2

I SPEAK of "all these years." At rare intervals it occurs to me that, in this current year of grace 1938, Ellen Glasgow is not any longer a young woman. I consider the arithmetical proofs of this fact, for a suitable while, with due deference; and I dismiss them as self-evident fallacies.

In every way except intellectually she is quite the youngest person I know of: she diffuses indeed enough youthful vitality to supply an orphan asylum; and when, not very long ago, in talking with me, she referred to her gray hair, it was with a sense of shock, and with some sudden surprise, that I perceived she was not talking nonsense. During the forty years I had known her, I had never noticed anything of the sort; and I promptly forgot the irrelevant hirsute detail, now that this glowing-eyed and wholly beautiful Boadicea—or it may be that my pedantic allusion refers to Bellona—began to tell me just what exactly she did think about one of our better-known literary critics, whose name is not either here or there. He had been civil enough; but his adulation was not vociferous. He ought to have said a great deal more about *Vein of Iron* after she had gone out of her way to be polite to him. And this, it developed, was but the most recent of his so many imbecilities; all which were duly catalogued.

I agreed with her, stifling my envy as best I might; for some reason or another, authors, howsoever arduously they may labor, simply do not ever acquire the knack of an authoress in combining polite sympathy for the feebleminded with excoriation; but I inferred, too, that gray hairs have not of necessity anything to do with the slackness of senescence. I perceived that Ellen Glasgow remained a young woman so far as went those several thousands of earthly matters which interest her very vividly, and which thus keep perpetual her youth.

3

Now, in chief, does Ellen Glasgow love dogs; and second only to dogs, all forms of animal life except human beings; and thirdly, humane letters. Here her range is wide; yet in all British and American literature she admires deeply but two women writers—one living and one dead. The dead one is Jane Austen.

In all persons who write as to current reading-matter the interest of Ellen Glasgow is cordial; she is not ever unkind to a book reviewer within earshot. She loves likewise old furniture; and philosophy in book form; and being made much of; and age-old gardens; and lavishness in her giftgiving; and gossip; and pessimism, to an extent which she occludes from her fiction, reserving the full force of it for her proposed autobiography; and detective stories; and every conceivable nature of large or small china figure which represents this or the other sort of dog. Of these last, she has a hundred or so. With an unfeminine fondness does she cherish, a bit even above the exploits of Lord Peter Wimsey or of Mr. Reginald Fortune or of M. Hercule Poirot, the brave novels of Alexandre Dumas; and she delights also to give a dinner party with all proper pomps and fanfaronades.

To the other side, she nurtures a trinity of dislikes. She deplores sentimentality except only when it is lavished upon dumb animals. Her fellow-creatures she does not love *en masse* with an entire cordiality; and even though she was raised in the best Presbyterian principles, her affection for Jehovah remains temperate.

That listing sounds rather miscellaneous, I admit. I mean only that through her joy in, or through her dislike of, these matters and a great many other matters, Ellen Glasgow continually rises in her private life to a sort of lyric intensity which is youth's self.

I mean, in brief, that I cannot recollect any single topic, howsoever commonplace or recondite, as to which her views are half-hearted, or uncertain, or, above all, uninteresting.

I mean too that, although she irradiates in her private life that same energy which informs her books—that energy which when directed by daring and cultivated with humility becomes genius—yet in both fields she remains always, quite incommunicably, "well-bred." Here is personality, a most vivid personality; and it is fortified, not veiled, by the traditions of Southern aristocracy.

As being that which somebody or another has called "a Virginian of the old school," I delight in the alliance which Ellen Glasgow embodies, because, separately, I incline to admire both the genius and the *grande dame,* as being strange rarities nowadays. But when I find the two combined in one person, then I applaud something resembling a miracle.

FOUR

1

AFTER the prefaces which, in preparing her Social History of the remarkable Commonwealth of Virginia, Ellen Glasgow had written for her revised novels were themselves revised, and were put together as a separate volume, in 1943, under the title *A Certain Measure*, then yet again did I find myself, upon at least two counts, at wide variance with her current dust wrapper, which described this book as "a penetrating discussion of prose fiction . . . in flawless prose." Without raising here my secondary objection (which was, of course, that no human being has ever written a paragraph, far less an entire volume, of flawless prose), it seemed to me that inasmuch as throughout *A Certain Measure* Ellen Glasgow's theme was herself, and her mental forays, and the evolution of her novels, the book counted as an autobiography of the writer's mind.

So I presently said as much, in the *New York Evening Post*, with a pleased consciousness that Ellen Glasgow now wished to be approached, not merely as a novelist, but as a social historian.

Somewhat as when Edward Gibbon had completed his *History of the Decline and Fall of the Roman Empire* (I remarked), he then published his *Memoirs of My Life and Writings*, so now that Ellen Glasgow has finished her revised series of those thirteen novels which, here to quote from their writer, "comprise, in the more freely interpretative form of fiction, a social history of Virginia from the decade before the Confederacy," she likewise has turned toward self-portrayal, in *A Certain Measure*.

It has been observed (to round out the analogue) that "in the matter of style, Gibbon took a great deal more pains with himself than he did with the empire." Whereas each volume of the history except only the earliest, it may be remembered, was printed from his first draft, he wrote out for the memoirs a half-dozen pleasingly different versions before deciding upon the preferred disguise in which to make friends with posterity. His memoirs, in brief, were the more congenially and the more studiously composed of his two masterworks. And just so, *A Certain Measure* is, by long odds, the most zestfully done of all the many adroitly phrased books by Ellen Glasgow. I believe it, in fact, to be, when regarded singly, the very best of her books; and to a reflective reader, by far the most interesting, because, to my finding, Ellen Glasgow here displays a personality more noteworthy than is that of any character in her Social History of Virginia.

2

TRULY, in the production of an autobiography the historian has an advantage hitherto denied. It is the chief peril of an historian's work that his art must lead him to impersonate knowledge which he, or it may be even she, in mere point of fact and through no stint of endeavor, does not possess. Most precariously does this become true when the historian needs to make plain some special type of character or of emotion about which—perhaps on account of the involved artist's sex or race or rearing, or it may be through an unthrifty adhesion to continence and respectable living—the historian does not know anything, except by report.

I have heard mentioned hereabouts the word "intuition"; and I have made bold to regard the word as a quite possible synonym for "humbug." The historian, in his more vivid passages of impressive and subtle analysis, is compelled very often to fake his writing, through mere lack of omniscience.

During the composition of a Social History of Virginia, "in the more freely interpretative form of fiction," Ellen Glasgow, of necessity, has not been able always to speak from her own natural point of view. She has needed to impersonate any number of quite other points of view, in her attempt to present a reasonably complete social structure.

She has thus been led to depict, not only the actions, but the emotions, of several young males under the influence of love, and the thoughts of a retired Protestant clergyman while awaiting his turn to be served in a bread line, and the retrospections, alike military and sociological and extra-marital, of a former Confederate general—in a noble passage which, quite rightly, has been picked out by Ellen

Glasgow as containing much of her most closely representative prose. She has delineated the resigned sentiments of a time-tamed husband toward his wife; the meditations of an uneducated and deferentially pious Negress; and a father's loving yet partly impatient thoughts concerning his headstrong, young married daughters.

One might name scores of yet other instances in which, as a social historian, Ellen Glasgow has found herself required to deal introspectively with affairs which were not always comprehensible to Ellen Glasgow through any vital experience—any more than was to Gibbon, let us say, the deplorably un-English temperament of the harlot-empress Theodora, or the moral standards of Mahomet, or the quaint zest with which quite a number of Early Christians appeared to enter the arena. —For to depict these alien mentalities was a part of the historian's job; and howsoever handsomely the task has been discharged, by each writer, it perforce had to be discharged through the aid of industry and of fancy, in default of knowledge.

3

In *A Certain Measure* this handicap has been removed, with results brightly delightful. Ellen Glasgow is here free to speak always in her own per-

son, and from her own point of view, about herself
and about the books by which she will be remembered; about human life in general; about her childhood, and about Southern gentlewomen, and
about Ellen Glasgow's methods of novel-writing,
and about (in great Mencken's once habitual
phrase) "the late Confederacy," and about a bevy of
Ellen Glasgow's pet philosophers ranging from John
Stuart Mill to Stuart P. Sherman.

She expounds, in short, as to almost all matters
which have concerned Ellen Glasgow during her
some-and-forty years of serene advancement, from
being as modern as Thomas Hardy, at a period when
modernity was hailed as being *fin de siècle,* toward a
more conservative state of grace in the Elysium of
our present-day American Academy of Arts and
Letters.

Her intellectual self-record thus takes form as a
surprisingly chameleon-like volume, by turns frank,
or seductive, or rich with shrewdness—being, when
the need rises, as bare as Euclid, as diffuse as Mrs.
Nickleby, or as neatly burnished as a carved fragment from Pater,—but at every moment the book
stays warmly human. It is all Ellen Glasgow just for
this once only very moderately diluted by the his-
trionics required of historians. Under the influence
of her personality, you, as you read, may agree or
disagree; you may find nourishment for some irrita-

tion in the presence of what appears to be arrogance now and then; but in any case (if you are reasonably intelligent) you will go on reading this unique epilogue to an enterprise without any precise parallel in Virginian history.

4

"In Virginian history," I needs repeat. —For still to pursue my analogue, I think that Ellen Glasgow's large panorama of the customs and failings and virtues of the State of Virginia, throughout the course of four generations, displays an inventiveness such as, to say the very least of it, appears not inferior to that which throughout Edward Gibbon's great history of the senescence of Rome goads the Reverend H. H. Milman, at the bottom of about every third page, into a chronic frenzy of expostulating footnotes. I believe that by means of her luminous and accurate prose the senescence of our Tidewater Virginia after the War Between the States has been interpreted from well-nigh every conceivable angle, in the light of humor, and of more than sufficiently sound knowledge, and of a loving if not always underisive sympathy, for the benefit of any such possible posterity as may yet outlive the combined labors of ballistics and patriotism.

And it follows that I do not applaud the result as

being fiction of the first quality. My point instead is that, when viewed properly, as a whole, the work of Ellen Glasgow is history of the first quality—history "in the more freely interpretative form of fiction."

FIVE

1

Such, then, was the tenor of my four "occasional" papers which commemorated, severally, the accession of Ellen Glasgow (in 1925, when *Barren Ground* was published) to a grant of some serious consideration as a writer; and the advance of Ellen Glasgow, in 1930, to the dignity of an attempted Collected Edition; and the rounding off of Ellen Glasgow's career when, between 1938 and 1943, she finally did put forth a definitive version of her better novels (along with their biographical epilogue, in *A Certain Measure*) as being "a Social History of Virginia from the decade before the Confederacy."

Now at this point I concede my inability, alike before and after the death of Ellen Glasgow, to think about her novels in common with other novels. She was too nearly my associate. Throughout some twenty years we each observed, as if under a microscope, just how the books of the other developed from embryons into published volumes; informally, we each contributed to the other's books: and it follows that I cannot pretend to appraise a fair number of her books by the rigid criteria of æsthetic values any more rigorously than my own books. In regard to both authors I am prejudiced.

We were friends for some forty-seven years, with an ever increasing intimacy; so that during the last twenty of these years I was privileged to observe at close quarters more aspects of Ellen Glasgow than ever, I am certain, were revealed to any other one person. We differed, cordially and without compromise, as to so very many matters that she delighted to foretell, with a grim enjoyment, my own lack of enjoyment if I survived her long enough to read that which she had written about me in her autobiography; yet we differed always without any rancor. We differed always—as she wrote to me, exactly three months before her death—"with the old friendship and sympathy," during the entire twenty years that each of us was a recognized part of the other's living.

For these reasons, now that Ellen Glasgow is dead, I cannot write about her without seeming either infatuated or disloyal—or quite possibly both. I have chosen, therefore, to leave unaltered, except for as much editing as appears to make more plain my meaning when I published the four articles included here, that which I wrote concerning Ellen Glasgow, and her novels, and her prefaces to them, while she was yet alive. I have not attempted to conceal the fact that, like any other intelligent critic, she esteemed the merits of Ellen Glasgow; nor the circumstance that, like every other writer whom I have known, she disliked any nature of fault-finding with her books.

"All that I ask," she used to remark, impartially, "is adulation."

And in thus speaking she voiced to perfection, I believe, that which has been the heartfelt requirement of every author since about 1407 B. C., when Moses-ben-Amram completed the Pentateuch with an impressive account of his own death and of his unexampled importance in the eyes of posterity.

2

In the approach to a Social History of Virginia, one travels without any such personal impedimenta as the recollections of twenty years; and there is no need to be considering diverse standards of creative art. Should a social history evince in its writing many, or indeed every one, of the auctorial virtues— by which I mean distinction and clarity, and beauty and symmetry, and tenderness and truth and urbanity—the fact is so much clear gain; and yet too it may be dismissed as a windfall: for the main question involved stays, after all, and among all possible byplays of inventiveness or ornamentation, whether or not the chronicle be vividly communicative, and comprehensive, and as factual in its core as a multiplication table.

No person who is tolerably familiar with Ellen Glasgow's native state will dispute the essential, the constant and the very vigorously conveyed actuality of her portrayal of Virginian life during her selected era. That merely is my point now that I have come to accept dead Ellen Glasgow, upon her own terms, as an historian; and as being pre-eminent among those so numerous persons who, ever since the remote times when Don Luis de Velasco instructed the hidalgos of Spain, through never so many "highly colored representations of the prosperous and cultural conditions of his people," and when Captain John Smith reanimated the old legend of Pocahontas, have one and all agreed to set forth the history of Virginia "in the more freely interpretative form of fiction."

Furthermore, I am so far incivic as to doubt if the beneficent and gracious commonwealth which, again and yet again, has honored me with a summons to jury service, and which annually favors me toward Christmas time with several tax bills, must of necessity survive in an always increasing splendor. I remember, it may be a bit morbidly, Assyria and Babylon and Poictesme and the present status of the people of Pericles.

Yet even should the worst befall, so that by-and-by only a few archæologists may remain interested in the doings of an extinct and half-legendary tribe called "Virginians," then, pair by pair, will the strong reading glasses of the professorial be turned toward the Collected Works of Ellen Glasgow (I like to think) in quest of sound information as to that lost people's customs and superstitions and their communal life for about eighty years or more—beside, as it were, the death-bed of that which was once an aristocracy and even, in some sort, a special civilization, now utterly perished.

3

"*Carpe diem*," I remark in my most polished scholastic manner, during the same instant that I feed into my typewriter a fresh sheet of paper.

—For the one world which I ever knew or cared about appears to be demolishing itself upon loud moral principles; and my one certainty as concerns the future is that I shall not very much like it. I infer that we can but make the utmost of our allotted to-day, as long as any daylight remains for us.

Meanwhile, our Virginian version of the history of Virginia, as one finds it begun by Don Luis de Velasco—and as it has been added to, in each generation, by the never so many other fine fiction mongers who have followed after him, alike in the Colony and in the State of Virginia, even down to the prime of Ellen Glasgow—that too survives to inspire us; it hinders despair's entrance into the sturdy Anglo-Saxon bosom of any true Virginian; and this composite romance is yet prompting us to live in a manner not unworthy of our titanic local forefathers, whose "free and valiant spirit," as Ellen Glasgow has phrased the affair, "gave birth to all that is free and valiant in our history [and has made] a country without a name the foremost republic in the world."

An Epilogue ⁊

AS TO OUR LIFE AND LETTERS

_____

Of beauty and of chivalry and of gray legions they spoke, and of a fallen civilization such as the world will not ever see again, and, for that matter, never did see; of a first permanent settlement, and of a Mother of Presidents, and of a republic's cradle, and of Stars and Bars, and of yet many other bygones, long ago at one with dead Troy and Atlantis, they babbled likewise, for interminable years, without ever, ever ceasing. The wind blew away their words as each word was spoken: still did they vocalize in the wind's teeth.

SPECIAL DELIVERY

1

*The scene is the writing room at Poynton Lodge,
within which this book began; and two Virginian
authors are there discovered midcourse in debate.*

*Their talk follows; and inasmuch as both speakers
bear the same surname, we may best distinguish between them as being the senior and the junior
phrase-vendor.*

JUNIOR:—And besides, sir, now that for your comfort's sake I am leaving you, in what more suitable
fashion could anybody end a book concerning the
State of Virginia and the notions of Virginia and the
customs of Virginia than by displaying in practice
the courtesy which upon all occasions a Virginian
evinces toward his fellow-Virginian?

SENIOR: I can understand your desire to advertise
your books without being wholly able to detect my
own special interest in this scheme—

JUNIOR: You will henceforward collect all royal-
ties upon them.

SENIOR: You speak, alas, of the infinitesimal. Nor
indeed do I comprehend just how you would have me
abet your project.

JUNIOR: It had been my hope that you, sir, if only
as being the first of all my reviewers, might grace

my departure from Poynton Lodge by expanding upon the remarks with which, in 1932, you honored my debut in print.

SENIOR: I can recall that as a favor to the Literary Guild I did review the book with which you began your auctorial career.—For in Virginia, as you have suggested, it is believed to be the duty of us older writers to encourage, verbally at any rate, our successors in time-wasting, no matter what must be our private opinion as to their inescapable doom and demerits. So I daresay that in your behalf I perjured myself politely, even though, as I can but confess, the precise nature of the balderdash which at this time—

JUNIOR: Oh, but, sir, this review of my first book which you then published was very far from being balderdash.

SENIOR: When I spoke as to the balderdash which either the one or the other of us published in 1932, I was not being egotistic. Yet since you have the clipping, do you let me read it.

JUNIOR: Most willingly, my dear sir, upon the sole condition that it be read aloud.

SENIOR: The request appears reasonable. So let us now discover whatever it was that, in 1932, I pretended to think about your first book, the name of which, I admit, at just this instant—

JUNIOR: It was called, sir, *These Restless Heads*.

2

SENIOR: Why, but, yes, to be sure. And under the heading "Some Objections to Branch Cabell," I remarked as to your first published volume, so this clipping reports:

For all that I wish for Branch Cabell all kinds of good luck, within such moderate limits of success as any human being can find endurable in a lifelong acquaintance, and for all that I have labored through his first book with a personal interest such as, of late years, I have not accorded to the work of any other beginning writer, yet has this book left me unpleasantly impressed. In a beginner, charity allows for much. Yet there is no hiding the fact that the author of *These Restless Heads* is truthful; he is even very much in earnest; and if there be any third form of self-indulgence equally damaging to literary success, I do not know of it.

Nor is this all which troubles me in this book. To me the verbarian and verbose Virginian who has written *These Restless Heads* appears to be over-fond of his dabblings in rhetoric. I note, for example, his reiteration of the refrain word "nonsense" (perhaps not inappropriately picked out) at the close of each section of the book—as well as a kindred juggling with the word "contentment" in the coda of those four sections which are devoted, without any such thin trickery as figures in the Prologue and Epilogue, to the writer's ever-present, omnivorous interest in himself. I observe such unrestrained instances of onomatopœia as "this flag's fleet, unflagging, flippity-flop, flapping" or the paronomasia of "like dead leaves scuttling and bustling aflutter to rustle in dusty gutters." I regard the elaborate building up of long rhapsodies and *tirades* in order that, the instant they reach completion, their architect may tumble them over. I lift gray eyebrows before an ubiquitariness of "prose rhythms," fashioned after the antiquated recipes of Professor George Saintsbury, as these verbal cates are exemplified again and yet again. And I decide that common-sense cannot but object to this handling of words as if they were diamonds.

These and yet many other instances of the *faux bon*—as we humanists by ordinary put it when we contemn whatsoever is admired by persons who do not admire us—I observe with disquiet. It seems to me that upon his filigree knickknacks Branch Cabell has wasted a superfluity of effort. Such rhetorical love-knots are at odds with our plain-spoken age; and one cannot but shrug over the infinite labor which, even nowadays, a beginning author can devote thus thriftlessly to the more intricate refinements of writing, almost as if in America the shaping of prose were a recognized form of art. We older and more considerate word-pedlars have been taught, a good while ago, by our readers in conjunction with our royalty statements, to write otherwise. We do not attempt, in Branch Cabell's pernickety phrase, "to guide the unicorn in double harness with the dray horse."

For the beginner's improvement, however, there is always hope; and "with time and experience, aided by the sympathetic appreciation of the reviewer," it may be that Branch Cabell may learn how to do better, in a fashion rather more modishly copied after *McGuffey's First Reader*. Meanwhile I could wish that the personality of this new writer were, to my personal taste, a bit more attractive. —For he betrays, over and yet over again, a weak-spirited acceptance of the off-chance that this universe may prove both kindly and comfortable such as no time-approved pessimist of my own more rigorously sophisticated era in letters can avoid finding repugnant. Branch Cabell, in brief, appears to enjoy life, howsoever soberly; he endorses, to every practical intent, the age-old rulings of human wisdom; and to the better class of American writers, for the last fifteen years or more, no such naïve equanimity has been permitted.

3

JUNIOR: The review runs somewhat more harshly than I had remembered it—

SENIOR: Here and there I may have misread a phrase or two, inasmuch as the time-faded clipping has become not wholly legible. Yet to the gist of it I adhere; and if only you had given heed to my warning you might have prospered with a deal more of luxuriance. But instead you continued a debauch in the writing of essays by publishing a volume of frank replies to the unsolicited correspondents who annoy all authors. It was an inspiration, in its own limited field, so happy that I wondered why I myself had not thought of it; but to the other side, you did not handle your inspiration with tact. —For it was in this book, of which the title, I confess, escapes me—

JUNIOR: You allude, I imagine, to *Special Delivery*, as I issued it in 1933.

SENIOR: With the irreverence which youth owes to age, you have been so punctilious as to interrupt me. Otherwise, one might have observed that in this

Special Delivery you admitted: "As I grow older, I find I am more than usual calm (without exactly completing Pet Marjorie's phrase) as to all questions of large social import. I burn with generous indignation over this world's pig-headedness and injustice at no time whatever."

JUNIOR: But no, sir, for that was in *These Restless Heads*.

SENIOR: The point is that it should not have been anywhere. It is the duty of every staunch American to burn always with a generous indignation at an instant's notice, even in the twinkling of a bed post; and more especially was this true during the beginning years of the Great Depression when you first began to publish. So the phrase stamped you irretrievably; it was quoted by some nine reviewers out of each ten who noticed your existence; for it revealed you as a mere fribbler. Nor did you at all help matters when, not long afterward, with a continuance in the same vein of futile irresponsibility, you addressed a parcel of letters to a number of once famous dead persons, which you called something or other—

JUNIOR: That was *Ladies and Gentlemen,* sir, and they were not letters but elegies—

SENIOR: The book's title annihilated you unheard. Into the reading-matter of the 1930's no gentry were admitted. —For this was in the heyday of serious

277

and painstaking studies of the mentally underprivileged, by their peers, in the proletarian novel. All the more modern and advanced authors of America, during the social-minded 1930's, had advanced some ninety years backward; and had thus regained the high standards of Mr. Thomas Ritchie of Tappahannock.

JUNIOR: Now but there, I submit, you abandon veracity in the pursuit of paradox.

SENIOR: Why, but not in the least: for during the 'thirties it became the true end of literature to seek out the violet in its lowly bed, in the avatar of unskilled labor, and to give its perfume to the light of day; to dilate upon the humble worth and unpretending merit of them that had been emigrants; and in short, to bestow upon the inefficient, the streetwalker, the gangster, and the share-cropper, the conspicuous position to which they were entitled. With the revived ardor of Charles Dickens, if with a perceptible absence of his or of any other sort of humor, the great and the glaring and the magnificent were denounced, after the time-approved methods of *Bleak House* and *Hard Times* and *Little Dorrit*, as being social evils caused by the capitalist system; and ladies and gentlemen (whensoever indeed an author could force his genius to touch upon a topic so uncongenial) were dismissed as not being consistent with any Marxian theory of perfection. You

278

could not possibly have selected for your book of elegies, as you call them, a title which was more repugnant to the spirit of the age.

JUNIOR: But have we ever bothered about the spirit of the age?

SENIOR: Not to the exact extent which would have gratified our publishers, perhaps. —For we, of necessity, have remained Virginians of the old school. It has been our fortune to belong, willy-nilly, to an age which perished some little while before we were born; and chance has thus led us to exist, somewhat as did your Peripatetic Episcopalian, in a planet to which we were not native.

JUNIOR: It remains possible that as yet I do not understand you.

4

SENIOR: I mean merely that the well-born Virginian who began life not long after the War Between the States is now seen to have been uncommonly lucky. Of the elegiac atmosphere in which he was reared, enough has been remarked elsewhere; it inoculated him; and it has thus happily enabled him, throughout the remainder of his living, to combine the spiritual uplift of martyrdom with an engaging lack of martyrdom's more customary physical discomforts.

Yet furthermore, as we have noted, while he was yet an infant confined to the nursery, the idea was quite firmly implanted in his mind, by his Negro mammy, that never was he in the wrong. It was the persons who rebuked his conduct that were in the wrong. And he has retained this idea. He has reached not merely manhood, but either his late middle life or his family section in the graveyard, without ever leaning so freakishly toward the whimsical as to conceive of himself as being, in any imaginable circumstances, mistaken; and with an equal infrequence has his fancy so far rioted as to depicture its owner as involved in misdoing.

We have seen likewise that, by his elders, the well-born Virginian of our era was tutored to revere himself as being the dispossessed heir to an all-perfect and all-admirable estate in the Old South. We were taught that we had been robbed; that our rights had been taken away from us at Appomattox; and that all our baronial desmesnes in a beauty-haunted and chivalrous Cloud-Cuckoo-Land had been demolished in the McLeans' front parlor. We in this way began to live with a cast-iron faith in our own rightness; with an ever-present sense of having been martyred by Northern fanatics; and with a conviction that all good and all glory were to be found in the past.

Nor of any one of these three illusions has time or—should you permit me yet again to plagiarize—

"time's stolid offspring, whom we name common-sense," been able to rid us, because the impressions of one's childhood and of one's youth remain ineradicable. That which, incessantly, we were taught before reaching manhood we must continue to believe forever in our hearts; so that even should our reason be convinced that some of if not all this teaching was incorrect, our hearts simply do not honor the argument with their attention. The heart—it is a striking reflection which I commend alike to all merely rational persons and to most orators—the heart has no ears.

So the well-born Virginian has retained his illusions willy-nilly; and because of them he has not figured to advantage in the field of material achievements, a field which he has entered only when necessity pushed him, and in which he has worked begrudgingly, because of these illusions. I do not mean, of course, that in farming and finance and road-building, and so on, the State of Virginia has failed to provoke its various chambers of commerce into an annual outburst of statistics and pride and elate prophesying. I mean, rather, that the well-born Virginian is not any longer in charge of Virginia.

It would seem, to the uninformed, a bit snobbish-sounding for me thus to be speaking so continually of "the well-born Virginian." And yet through what other phrase can I distinguish with justice between the unhorsed Virginian Cavalier—as I once termed him more loosely—and his civic superiors? To us two, at any rate, it is no secret that most of our present-day pre-eminent Virginians have climbed to their well-merited success from out of that villenage of white families who, in the faraway days when Virginia was ruled by an oligarchy of planters, were ignored politely, without any comment, as belonging to one or another inferior caste. Our current leaders, in brief, where they were not imported from other states, have risen from the middle classes or else from the lower classes of Virginia, alike in commerce and politics and religion and letters and education and in yet other commendable branches of human activity.

I do not say this in dispraise. I speak instead with the fair-mindedness of Madam Esmond Warrington. Like Madison and Monroe and Washington, our leaders are self-made persons who have performed to admiration the task of their self-making; and who are discharging their present-day high functions with competence. They are right-thinking Virginians who in their every public utterance continue to look forward, through a handsome vista of rhetoric, toward the unparalleled future of a commonwealth than which and so forth and so on. Virginia has need of these brisk and anæsthetic leaders; and to that need they one and all are responding conscientiously, if without any especial distinction.

So my point here is merely that the well-born Virginian of our own era is not, and has never been, able to look forward. He has not even looked, with any large interest, at his current surroundings. —For we were taught always to look backward, toward the glories of which we had been dispossessed at Appomattox. And to each one of us it has seemed unjust that he, the defrauded heir to a peerage in the Old South, should have to work for his living. I do not mean that, of necessity, we have ever admitted this fact, even to ourselves; but at our hearts' bottom such has been our belief.

It has followed that, by and large, we have labored without gusto in the field of material achievements; and that—still speaking by and large—we as a generation have failed there.

The poverty no less than the indolence of the well-born Virginian, as a class, remains notorious; for it is not only in the Northern Neck that the aristocrat, far fallen from seigneury, has been earning a haphazard livelihood ever since the one war which he has found to be estimable. So has it come about that most of our contemporaries who, as we have phrased it, may define themselves without any thought of vainglory, or of being contradicted, as belonging to the best families of Virginia have failed, by all earthly standards.

5

JUNIOR: You speak with conviction. And yet do you leave me unpersuaded that from the fact of our generation's having failed, by all earthly standards —an event which I shall neither grant nor deny— the deduction needs follow that we have been uncommonly lucky.

SENIOR: You incline to regard the well-born Virginian, I submit, without weighing properly the fine epigraph with which you have prefaced one of your own books. "To look at the man is but to court deception . . . for no man lives in the external truth, among salts and acids, but in the warm, phantasmagoric chamber of his brain, with the painted walls and the storied windows."

JUNIOR: I take your meaning, I believe, sir, for all that you speak with a demure politeness which your associates have learned to distrust. You would have me remember that, even from the first, you and I have lived in this manner; and that we have differed from our fellow-Virginians only through the circumstance that we perceived ourselves to be thus imprisoned.

SENIOR: Should we not say more wisely, "to be thus sheltered"? —For very truly the fortress of the well-born Virginian is impregnable. As Hernandez has told us, no power in nature can upset the faith of a

Virginian of the old school as to the myths among which he was reared, and of which he needs to be worthy. No power can shake his belief in his own eternal rightness, as Mrs. Nelson or some one or the other of her inferior dark fellow-angels in heaven has made firm that belief. Nor, as Ellen Glasgow has shown, can any known power take away, from the well-born Virginian, that ever-sustaining sense of moral uplift which he gets out of being chivalrous at no matter what costs to himself, or to other persons either. He thus lives, it may be, in a fool's paradise; yet I do not know that this earth of ours affords any other sort of paradise; and for this reason I adjudge a Virginian of the old school to be uncommonly lucky. And I find him likewise to be admirable in that, to quote from my esteemed friend Mr. Reginald Fortune, he does not ever put up with any nonsense from facts. Like your own Smire, he knows that for humankind the dream is the one true reality,—that dream which commands him continually, as Mrs. Nelson expressed it, to let people see his raising,— even that brave rigorous dream which guided Robert E. Lee toward a self-imposed exile in Lexington.

JUNIOR: Inasmuch as you have paid me the compliment of citing several of my books, I may fairly retaliate in kind. I think that you, sir, would attempt to preserve the sentiments of Virginia without sharing in the belief which begot them; and that you would yet cling to gods in whom you retain no faith. You would have us believe, in fine, that the way of Virginia is the way of Ecben. You would tell us that, to the impertinences of common-sense, the gray, or it may be the bald-headed, but still chivalrous Virginian of our own class and generation, which has achieved nothing in particular, can always reply, even as did King Alfgar in the Garden between Dawn and Sunrise:

"Yet am I content. —For I have served that dream which I elected to be serving. It may be that no man is royal, and that no god is divine, and that our mothers and our wives have not any part in holiness. Oh, yes, it very well may be that I have lost honor and applause, and that I take destruction, through following after a dream which has in it no truth. Yet my dream was noble; and its nobility contents me."

SENIOR: What author can stay unbiased when his own words are being quoted verbatim and almost seriously? Yes: I incline to agree with you that the Alfgar of the old legend which I once paraphrased may have prefigured the well-born Virginian of to-day; and I grant likewise that through this adroit answer the Virginian, whom in this book we have criticized somewhat variously, has now got the better of us both.

EXPLICIT

286